TRAIN TRANSFORM TRANSITION

A Strategic Approach to
the Life You Deserve

GERALDA LARKINS

Copyright © 2017 GERALDA LARKINS | IMPART KINGDOM

Prepared by: Ebony Nicole Smith | Exclusively4Clergy | www.EbonyNicoleSmith.com

Editor: A.B. Brumfield | Crimson Cross Publishing

Cover: Dynasty Cover

All rights reserved.

ISBN-13: 978-0-692-85495-2

All rights reserved. This book is protected by the copyright laws of the United States of America. This book may not be copied or reprinted for commercial gain or profit. The use of short quotations or occasional page copying for personal or group study is permitted and encouraged. Permission will be granted upon request. Scriptures taken from the Holy Bible, New International Version®, NIV®. Copyright © 1973, 1978, 1984, 2011 by Biblica, Inc.™ Used by permission of Zondervan. All rights reserved worldwide. www.zondervan.com The "NIV" and "New International Version" are trademarks registered in the United States Patent and Trademark Office by Biblica, Inc.™ Scripture taken from the New King James Version®. Copyright © 1982 by Thomas Nelson. Used by permission. All rights reserved.

DEDICATION

I dedicate this book to every Kingdom Visionary, to my family, to my friends, to my leaders, and my followers. I dedicate this to Chris. I dedicate this to God for revealing what it means to train, transform, and transition!

Greater works you will do, because Greater is in you!

Your Visionary Strategist,

Geralda Larkins

GERALDA LARKINS

TABLE OF CONTENTS

FORWARD 1

INTRODUCTION 5

TRAIN

PLANS INTERRUPTED	11
REVELATION	23
KNOW GOD	31
KNOW YOURSELF	45
KNOW YOUR SPHERE	55

TRANSFORM

THE BUSINESS OF CHANGE	71
REAL TRANSFORMATION	79
RENEWING YOUR MIND	93
TRAINING PLAN	101

TRANSITION

THE COURAGE ZONE	113
WHAT IS TRANSITION	121
DON'T LOOK BACK	129
TRANSITION BY FAITH	137
FAITH AND VISION	143
FOCUS AND FORGET	159

STRATEGIC TRAINING PLAN 167

NOTES 170

GERALDA LARKINS

FORWARD

For My thoughts are not your thoughts, Nor are your ways My ways, declares the Lord, For as the heavens are higher than the earth, so are my ways higher than your ways and my thoughts than your thoughts," Isaiah 55:8-9.

The bible constantly reminds us that God has a way of doing things that will ultimately equip us for the planned work He has predestined for us to accomplish. God leaves no stone unturned concerning our lives. It is His will to mold us into who He has designed us to be. That's why *Train Transform Transition* is so vital. Geralda walks you through a Spirit-led strategic process, which will position you to yield supernatural results in every area of your life. This approach will allow you to achieve real success, not measured by the world's standards but by God's metric standard.

God's standard of success is not at face value, it's not one dimensional, and it's not based on your career, education, your money or your connections. True success is living out God's plan for your life without compromising your convictions, utilizing your gifts, talents and skills in a way that's pleasing to Him. By this, you bring glory to His name and exhibit the traits of a true agent of change. It's running in such a way that you won't grow weary. It's walking in such a way that you won't faint. It's producing good fruit that will last. And it's birthing what you conceive and knowing how to nurture it to maturation.

Many want success or can see the vision but don't understand or aren't willing to go through the process to be able to see it through. The bulk of the development reveals who we think we are verses who God has called us to be; and where we are verses where God wants us to be -- spiritually, emotionally and professionally. *Train Transform Transition* will help you navigate through these various phases of your life.

This strategic approach has changed the lives of countless men and women entrepreneurs who have attended Geralda's networking events as well as a multitude of viewers of her online talk show, *Train Transform Transition*. She speaks to various Kingdom Visionaries and offers Kingdom Essentials to help in life, in ministry and in the market. As a successful businesswoman, a dedicated church member, Pastor, administrator, loving mother, faithful wife, sister and spiritual daughter, I have personally and professionally witnessed her heart, character, integrity and passion. Geralda is selfless and has a deep desire to equip and steer other visionaries to succeed. She understands the weight and the magnitude of their success, because when one succeeds we all succeed for we are helpers one to another.

So if you're ready to experience real spiritual growth, real change, and real success that transcends generations and makes an eternal impact for the Kingdom of God, this book will prepare you for success. Do not become impatient with the process, submit to it, and experience a great return. Preparation is never a waste of time. It is the key to fulfilling God's purpose for your life.

Apostle Samantha Williams

Soul Harvest Creative Praise Ministries

GERALDA LARKINS

INTRODUCTION:

- Train: to learn a particular skill or type of behavior through practice and teaching over a period of time.

- Transform: to make a thorough or dramatic change in form, appearance, or character.

- Transition: to go, move, or pass from one position, state, stage, to another.

Train. Transform. Transition. Learn. Change. Go. Too many people live their whole lives wandering aimlessly, searching for fulfillment, asking themselves, "Am I living out my purpose?". They feel hopeless and disconnected from God and the plan He has for them. They have a deep desire for forward progress, but do not seem to know where to start or are too afraid to take a step in a new direction. Whether shackled by bad relationships, financial hardships, illness, past failures, or job dissatisfaction, the abundant life Christ promises is not a reality for many, but rather an elusive dream.

This book will help you to understand that God's vision for your life cannot manifest through wishful thinking. God's vision for your life can only manifest through strategic faith and consistent action. You need a strategy. God has a strategy, a big plan of action that will lead us to the life we deserve. His strategy involves our actions. It is His work and His strategy, but in His unbelievable grace He puts it into effect through us. What are the actions God gives us to do as part of His strategy? We are to train, transform, transition. We are to learn, change, and go.

Learn what? What am I changing into? Where am I going? These are very real questions that the Holy Spirit will begin to answer for you as you prayerfully read through this book. This book will teach you that as you train in the things of God, you will be transformed into who God calls you to be, and then empowered to transition into the life you were predestined to enjoy. The life you deserve. It is the abundant life that Christ died for you to possess, *"I have come that they may have life, and that they may have it more abundantly"* (John 10:10). What is this abundant life? It is a life of spiritual forward progress or, in other words, a life of achievement and success. It is a full life, a life of realizing your dreams and achieving victory. It is a life of blessing, hope, and promise.

As a Visionary Strategist, my goal is to help cultivate the vision God places in the hearts of His people and develop a strategy to attain it. Like I said before, God's strategic plan is already given to us in His word, but we must do our part, we must train, transform, transition. Train Transform Transition is a strategic approach to your destiny. You will receive revelation into timeless spiritual disciplines that when implemented strategically, will ultimately grow your faith, build your relationship with God, and give you the confidence needed to achieve abundant life. I will explain the train, transform, transition process in more detail in the pages to come, then help you develop a specific plan that works for you.

Just as business success depends on effective strategic planning and execution, God, through His Word, gives us strategies to lead us to the abundant life we deserve. God's well thought out strategies reveal His character and His relentless determination to return us back to our rightful place as sons, royalty, a kingdom of priests who rule, dominate, regulate and legislate on the earth as it is in heaven. This book is for Kingdom Visionaries, unapologetic followers of Jesus Christ that have a strong desire to walk in their purpose and who are ready to meet their spiritual goals to achieve success.

So grab a pen and some paper, your favorite snack (*I learn better with munchies*), as I call this meeting to order. You are about to embark on a strategic planning meeting for your life.

TRAIN

Heavenly Father, as Your people read the pages of this book, I pray that You open the eyes of their hearts to see the wonderful truths of Your Word which brings abundant life. Shine Your holy light which breaks through the darkest parts of the human soul to bring revelation, wisdom, and understanding. Give them the faith to move mountains, the power to overcome obstacles, and the grace to endure to eternity. Shift our thinking, our desires, and our choices that we may do all those things that are pleasing to You. We thank You for the hope that abounds in knowing You, Christ our God, our hope of glory. We give You all the glory, honor and praise, in Jesus' name. Amen.

GERALDA LARKINS

CHAPTER ONE

PLANS INTERRUPTED

"In their hearts humans plan their course, but the LORD establishes their steps" (Proverbs 16:9). I plan everything. I have been a planner my whole life. All through school my planner was my lifeline. In college, I loved getting the syllabus and mapping out exactly what it was going to take to do well in a class. My whole life was based on a series of goals and objectives to reach my personal definition of *success*. Every year, as long as I can remember, I would make lists for my lists, and it felt so good to put a check or a line through a task completed. Graduate high school - check. Graduate college - check. Land a great job – check. Own a home - check. Get married - check. Have a baby – check. On the outside, I was measuring up pretty well to my own standard for success. On

the outside, I was accomplishing more than the statistics said I would ever achieve. On the outside, I was the poster child for the American dream. On the inside, however, was a whole other ugly reality.

Buried in between all my accomplishments were things that I never planned for. I never planned for my father to disappear from my life when I was three years old and become a figment of my imagination. I never planned to be a victim of sexual abuse at six years old. I never planned for my mother to be murdered when I was sixteen years old and leave me and my siblings orphaned. I never planned to be homeless at nineteen years old. I never planned to be divorced at twenty-three years old. I never planned to remarry, only to get divorced again at twenty-eight years old. I never planned to be a single mother. I never planned for my only son to have special needs. None of these things were in my plans. I dealt with these unplanned things the only way I knew how; I made another plan.

I never pondered on those challenging circumstances for too long. I never wanted to dwell on them, it was too painful. I never gave myself time to reflect on those matters and learn whatever lesson I was to glean from them. I do not even remember praying about them, I would just revert to my default process of planning, striving, achieving, falling, failing, breaking down, getting back up and planning again. The cycle just continued. But all of these circumstances had a profound impact on me. Brick by brick, I put up a barricade around my heart so as not to get hurt. I would put up boundaries to control my surroundings and maintain the appearance that I was ok. But I was a broken soul. A broken soul trying to live in a broken world can only lead to more brokenness. I saw the world from a broken state and this affected how I viewed people, how I viewed myself, and how I viewed God.

Part of my plan always included going to church. I knew I needed to attend church, not because I knew God, but because that was just what "good" people did. I remember being "saved" at twelve years old. One of the ushers grabbed my hand and led me to the alter. The preacher laid hands on my head and shouted out a fiery prayer. If you grew up in an old-school, Pentecostal, holiness church like I did, you already knew what was expected of you at that moment. You had to either cry or faint. I chose to faint. I fell back on cue, they put a sheet over me and the congregation broke out in praise and in tongues of fire.

I always enjoyed doing what people expected of me. I craved for the praise and the accolades that came from pleasing people. So, my church life was a works-based existence filled with emotional highs and lows that never quite satisfied the deep longing within me for "more". Left unsatisfied, church became less and less of a priority on my list. With every passing year, I would continue to plan out my life, trying to fill the void that just grew deeper and deeper.

In 2007 along came baby Oliver. Unplanned. By this time, I was on my second marriage and life was growing even more difficult. I was searching for love in all the wrong places. My ex and I were both selfish people and we had not learned how to disagree well. I was trying to love my spouse, but I did not respect him or myself. Fight after fight, with both of us hitting lower and lower below the belt, completely exasperated, and at a loss as to what to do, I left the marriage. I moved out. Everything was spiraling out of control. I had to get back in control of my life. Time for a new plan, however, it was not just about me anymore. I had a son whom I loved very much; a son I did not have very much patience for.

I had to be there for him and love him unconditionally, but my self-esteem was at its lowest point. I did not love myself, so how could I possibly love my baby? All I knew to do was make a plan for his life, but even that was not working out. Oliver was diagnosed with Autism. Unplanned. Now I had to deal with a barrage of doctors, therapists, nutritionists, medicines, and supplements to find some way to "fix" him. My plans resulted in constant disappointment and frustration. My plans no longer gave me the sense of control I needed. I felt anxious all the time. My confidence was shocked to its core. How did my life become so ugly? What kind of God would allow me to get to this point?

I remember one night, sitting alone in my apartment, I cried out to God in a prayer for help. I cried all night. Even with my eyes closed the thoughts of failure, hurt, defeat, and shame continued to replay over and over in my head. The very next day, I ran into an old friend from high school at the grocery store and we exchanged phone numbers. During one of our daily girl-friend chit chats, she asked if we could pray at the end of the call. I was confused, but of course I obliged. That was the "right" thing to do. The next day she suggested we go church-hopping. Even more confused, I agreed to go. Then I remembered that my dear, sweet, step-sister, Samantha Williams, was now pastoring the little old-school, Pentecostal, holiness church I grew up in. She would always invite the family to come to Sunday service, but none of us had an interest in going back. I thought to myself that Samantha would be happy to see we finally made it out to visit her church. Then I strategized within myself that I would get to please two people with one stone. So, I made plans to visit Soul Harvest Creative Praise Ministries. From that point on, my life has never been the same.

I will never forget the day when God revealed Himself to me. It was during my second visit to Soul Harvest Creative Praise Ministries. Church service was held in a small park recreation center and with only about ten chairs. My friend and I entered and took our seats and Samantha was once again happy to see us. She sang a few worship songs, prayed, and began to preach a sermon from a very common passage in the bible about a woman at the well. The encounter between Jesus and the Samaritan woman is the longest recorded conversation with the Lord in scripture.

John chapter four tells the story of how Jesus, tired from his travels, decides to take a break at a well and wait for his disciples to go get food. When a Samaritan woman appeared with her water jar in hand, Jesus made a simple yet profound request: *"Will you give me a drink?"* (John 4:7). I have heard this story many times from various pulpits, but this time it was as if Jesus came all the way from Heaven and waited for me to get to church that day just so He could have a life-changing conversation with me. Unplanned.

The Samaritan woman and I had a lot in common. Samaritans were seen as "unworthy" to the Jews, they did not get along, neither did they ever speak to one other. I, too, felt unworthy, rejected, and could not get along with anyone around me. I did not know how to communicate and my emotions always got the best of me. Having had five husbands and now living with a man who was not her husband, the Samaritan woman was an "outcast" in her community. To avoid people, she chose to draw water from the well at noonday instead of the cooler hours of the morning.

I, too, felt like an outcast in my family. After several failed relationships, now going on my second divorce, and transitioning from wife to being a single mother, my siblings jokingly call me "baby-momma" or "J-lo", aka *successful, but can't keep a man*. Afraid of being talked about, I kept to a small circle friends just to feel safe and in control at all times. Can you relate? Have you ever felt unworthy or like an outcast? I asked myself, why would Jesus decide to speak with me. What could this popular, well-liked, famous Rabbi possibly see in me? What did I have that could be of any value to Jesus? Just like the Samaritan woman, my heart responded, *"How can you ask me for a drink?"* (John 4:9). I wished Jesus would just stop talking to me because Him talking to me kept reminding me of just how unworthy I was. I had nothing to offer Him. Like the Samaritan woman, all I had was an empty vessel – a broken heart. The emotional hurt caused by past relationships, bad decisions, and disappointments caused cracks in my vessel, wounds and pain in my heart that no man or plan had been able to heal. I was scared, insecure, unsure, skeptical, tired, and broken, but Jesus kept drawing me to Himself.

In His grace and mercy, Jesus made me a proposition, *"If you knew the gift of God, and who it is who says to you, "Give me a drink," you would have asked Him, and He would have given you living water"* (John 4:10). Like the Samaritan woman, Jesus' offer peaked my interest. *"...Where can you get this living water?"* I was thirsty. That is exactly how I would describe the longing in my soul. Thirst. Thirst is defined as a feeling of needing or wanting to drink something to sustain life, a strong desire, a craving, a yearning, a hunger for something. Mankind is in a constant state of seeking and searching. We are always in restless pursuit of something, anything that will bring us a sense of fulfillment, success, and happiness. But Jesus is telling us that there is a place where this inner thirst can be satisfied. Sensing my fear and doubt, Jesus followed up with a bold promise, *"Those who drink the water I give will never be thirsty again. It becomes a fresh, bubbling spring within them, giving them eternal life"* (John 4:14).

Finally, the answer to my prayers! What I had been thirsting for all along was "living water". In another passage, Jesus says, *"Let anyone who is thirsty come to me and drink. Whoever believes in me, as Scripture has said, rivers of living water will flow from within them"* (John 7:37–38). Living water is the supernatural substance that Christ gives to bring and sustain life. Living water is the indwelling of the Holy Spirit. Jesus says if we only knew the gift of God, the gift of Heaven, the gift of eternity and all the supernatural benefits we are entitled to as citizens of Heaven, we would ask for living water, the Holy Spirit, and He would be given to us. Living water not only satisfies our inner thirst, but it gives us eternal life. We get to experience Heaven on earth. Not a bad deal, huh? So, if you are tired of living the same old life and you want to finally quench that relentless urge raging deep down inside of you, then will you cry out like the Samaritan woman and as I did that faithful Sunday, *"Please, sir, give me this water! Then I'll never be thirsty again..."* (John 4:15). Will you say that?

When I got the revelation of Christ that Sunday, I did in fact ask Him to come live in me and quench my thirst. I had to surrender my life for His life. Unfortunately, many people want their thirst quenched on their own terms. We want the easy way out, we do not want to work hard for it, and we think we are entitled to it. If you want living water, then you must understand that you cannot receive it in your old mindset, you need a new mind (Philippians 2:5). You cannot receive living water in your old way of life, you need a new life (2 Corinthians 5:17). You cannot carry living water in your old stony heart; you need a new heart (Ezekiel 36:26). You cannot bring your own will, your own desires, or your own stipulations to the table (Psalm 40:8). This is not a negotiation! We have made a mess of things because of rebellion and self-reliance. We have taken the ways that seem right to us, based on our own knowledge, our own wisdom, our own plans, and our own strength, and in the end it has led to nothing but death (Proverbs 14:12). We must start to see things differently (2 Corinthians 4:18).

For us to start anew, Jesus must confront us with the truth and the reality of our sin just like He did the Samaritan woman (John 4:16). Like her, we will do everything we can to avoid the truth, change the subject, and shift the focus from our sin because it is too painful to deal with. The Samaritan woman tried to steer Jesus away from dealing with her sin when she said, *"I know the Messiah is coming--the one who is called Christ. When he comes, he will explain everything to us."* (John 4:25). That is a *'yeah, yeah, alright, get off me, you can't judge me, only God can judge me, He knows my heart'* type of answer. But God knows just the right time to give us the grand revelation of Himself, and it is this revelation that will catapult us into our destiny. *"Then Jesus declared, "I, the one speaking to you, I am he."* (John 4:26).

CHAPTER TWO

REVELATION

New Testament scholar William Barclay said, *"There are two revelations in Christianity: the revelation of God and the revelation of ourselves."* In other words, through faith in Jesus Christ, you will come to know God and know yourself. This knowledge will be revealed to you. There is a difference between information and revelation. You can study a whole lot of information about God and about yourself, but if you have no revelation, it will not result in real transformation. When God gives us the gift of revelation, He turns the information we received in our natural mind into spiritual knowledge received by our spirit man. Our spirit bears witness to the revelation and wisdom is released.

Wisdom is the ability to apply knowledge. Our soul, which houses our intellect, receives wisdom from our spirit and is provoked to exercise its free will to take appropriate action. Our bodies just do what it is told to do. No matter how much information we study, if the information never turns into revelation, it has no ability to stimulate us to transformational action. But through revelation, we can be quickened by God in our spirit to take appropriate action toward our divine destiny.

What is revelation? Revelation is defined as a surprising and previously unknown fact, an eye-opener, a supernatural disclosure from God to humans, an act of revealing or communicating divine truth. When something is revealed to you, you now have an awareness, a consciousness, knowledge, and understanding of something which was previously hidden from you. Proverbs 29:18 says, *"Where there is no revelation, people cast off restraint."* The King James Version reads, *"Where there is no vision, the people perish."* Translated, the word revelation literally means *vision*.

We also see the word *vision* in 1 Samuel 3:1, *"The boy Samuel ministered before the LORD under Eli. In those days the word of the LORD was rare; there were not many visions."* Here, the passage associates vision with *a word from the Lord*. So, what Solomon is really saying in Proverbs 28:19 is that where there is no revelation, vision, or the Word of God - people perish. Translated, the word *perish* means to loosely stumble, cast off restraint, or to run wild. It is the same word used in Exodus 32:25 to describe how the Israelites totally lost it when they worshipped the golden calf: *"Moses saw that the people were running wild and that Aaron had let them get out of control and so become a laughingstock to their enemies."* We need revelation to avoid stumbling through life. Revelation keeps us from running wild and running off of God's predestined course for us.

Revelation comes from God, it is one of the ministries of the Holy Spirit. One of the purposes of the Holy Spirit is to reveal to us *"What no eye has seen, what no ear has heard, and what no human mind has conceived, the things God has prepared for those who love him—these are the things God has revealed to us by his Spirit. The Spirit searches all things, even the deep things of God."* (1 Corinthians 2:9-10). Jesus also tells us in John 16:13, *"But when he, the Spirit of truth, comes, he will guide you into all the truth. He will not speak on his own; he will speak only what he hears, and he will tell you what is yet to come."* The

Holy Spirit reveals the plan of God for our lives. The Holy Spirit reveals what God is saying and tells us what our future holds.

Like we have already established, revelation means vision. Vision is also defined as the ability to see, conceive, visualize, or picture. Bishop T.D. Jakes said, *"If you can conceive the invisible, you can achieve the impossible."* I heard a story about three bricklayers working beside each other on a wall. Someone came up to the first one and said, "What are you doing" "What's it look like I am doing?" he replied sarcastically, "I am laying bricks!" The man asked the next guy on the wall what he was doing. He said, "Can't you see what I am doing? I am building a wall." Then the last man was asked what he was doing. He exclaimed, "I am building a great cathedral for God!" Who do you think will do the best quality work and be the hardest worker? The one with vision.

Pastor Rick Warren says, *"Perhaps the most powerful aspect of vision is that it changes your way of thinking, which in turn changes the way you live."* Vision is not only what we see, but it is also the way in which we see. Our vision can be impaired if there is a problem with our lens. Jesus spent a great deal of time talking about the heart and the eye in His sermon on the mount. He talks about the level of darkness of the eye (Matthew 6:22) and having a splinter in the eye (Matthew 7:5). It is clear that Jesus is talking about the lens of the heart.

In Ephesians 1:18, Paul writes, *"I pray that the eyes of your heart may be enlightened in order that you may know the hope to which he has called you, the riches of his glorious inheritance in his holy people."* Paul prays that the eyes of our heart would be enlightened. In other words, while we perceive with our natural eyes, we really see with our hearts. Our minds receive images from our eyes but our heart interprets these images and comes up with a conclusion of what is real. If our hearts are filled with bitterness, envy, unforgiveness, resentment, jealousy, shame, hurt, defeat, rejection, and other darkness, then we will have a distorted view of reality. What we perceive as truth and what is really truth could be two completely different things.

Jesus says, *"You will know the truth and the truth will make you free."* (John 8:32). Jesus is saying, you will understand what is real and that will free you to live the abundant life I died for you to have. You do not have to live a life weighed down by the hurts of your past. God wants us to see and understand what truth really is. Truth is the way things really are—not the way we think they are, would like them to be, or wish they were. Truth is reality from God's point of view and you need clear vision to see the truth. If you want to have the freedom to be who God has created you to be and enjoy the life Jesus died for you to have, then you have to see and comprehend the truth.

When the eyes of your heart are opened by the Spirit of God, you become what I call a Kingdom Visionary. A Kingdom Visionary is an unapologetic follower of Jesus Christ, who has a strong desire to walk in their purpose and bring transformation to others. Kingdom Visionaries cultivate a relationship with God and through an intimate relationship, God releases revelation. Kingdom Visionaries live by revelation not by religion. Kingdom Visionaries act on revelation. They live strategically and intentionally, applying the Word of God. Kingdom Visionaries purpose to do something meaningful with their lives to leave a legacy of God's glory in the earth. Kingdom Visionaries love their work because they see the big picture. One of the greatest assets of a Kingdom Visionary is vision. With it, they stand out from the crowd and experience supernatural results in every area of their lives.

How do we get vision? How do we get revelation? We pray and

ask God for it. Paul says in Ephesians 1:7, *"I keep asking that the God of our Lord Jesus Christ, the glorious Father, may give you the Spirit of wisdom and revelation, so that you may know him better."* To experience the life you deserve, you need a vision of who God is and of who you are in Him. You also need a vision of the specific purpose God created you for. You need a vision of God as your Heavenly Father. You need a vision of who you are in Christ, His beloved child. You also need a vision of your sphere of influence, your purpose, what God has specifically called you to fulfill in the earth. Without a clear vision of God, self, and sphere, you can never attain the abundant life you deserve, the fullness of all that Christ purchased for you on the cross. Therefore, you must train on these three specific points: God, self, and sphere.

To train means to learn. Learning about God, yourself, and your sphere will position you to receive revelation in each of these very critical areas of life. When you take action on the revelation God gives you, consistently through practice, you gain new thoughts and new behaviors. The Apostle Paul said, *"Physical training is good, but training for godliness is much better, promising benefits in this life and in the life to come."* (1 Timothy 4:8). So, let the training begin.

CHAPTER THREE

KNOW GOD

A revelation of God always precedes us stepping out on faith to do something out of the norm. Let us again remember the Samaritan woman. When she received the revelation of who Christ was, she was compelled to leave her water jar, face the very neighbors she was hiding from, and tell them the Good News: *"Come, see a man who told me everything I ever did. Could this be the Christ?"* (John 4:29). We too need a revelation of God to propel us to do the very things we are afraid to do. We need a vision of God because from our human vantage point things could seem too great for us. We need the Word of God because our words do not give us the peace we need to move out into the deep. With man it is impossible, but with God all things are possible (Matthew 19:26). God has to reveal Himself in order to push us out of our comfort zone and do something new, like start a new business, launch a new ministry, write the book, lead a movement, or even lead a nation.

When Moses was about to lead the nation of Israel into the Promise Land, the enormity of the assignment weighed heavily on him. He had to lead this stubborn and rebellious nation out of slavery in Egypt, deal with all their complaining and grumbling, as well as face the reality of their enemies standing by ready to wipe them out. Moses went to God all stressed out, asking how was it going to happen, who was going to help, and what would it be like on the other side? Even after all of God's promises and all the signs and wonders Moses had witnessed, Moses still made one of the most profound appeals to God ever found in scripture: *"Now show me your glory."* (Exodus 33:18). In other words, Moses prayed for God to reveal who the great I AM was. Moses had a thirst to know God, His character, nature, and attributes. If Moses needed a vision of God to complete his assignment and operate effectively in his sphere, then we too need a vision of God in order to accomplish everything God calls us to do.

Jesus said, *"If you knew the gift of God, and who it is who says to you, "Give me a drink," you would have asked Him, and He would have given you living water."* (John 4:10). As we learned earlier, thirst for greatness and success is only satisfied by the living water Christ gives. This passage tells us that for us to ask for the living water we so desperately need, we need to know the gift of God and who God is. Jesus says, knowing this will compel us to ask for living water. The revelation of God reveals our need for Him, and prompts us to ask for living water.

If you only knew God. Do you know God? Who is God? Beyond what you have read about Him in the bible or beyond what you have heard about Him through testimonies of others, do *you* know God? Most believers give a knee-jerk response like, "Of course I know God. I'm saved, so therefore I know Him. I said the prayer and the preacher laid hands on me, so I know Him." Others may say, "I believe in God so that means I know God." Being saved and knowing God are two different things. Being saved is simply an introduction to God. But knowing God is a whole other matter. What does it mean to *know* God?

Knowing God is more than being saved and going to church every week. There are a lot of people that are saved and go to church that do not know God. In 1 Samuel chapter two, we read the story of the Prophet Samuel. Samuel was brought to the temple as a toddler by his mother to be raised by the Chief Priest Eli. Samuel lived, slept, and served in the temple. He was a good boy, admired and respected by the people. Eli had two sons who also worked in the temple along with Samuel. But Eli's sons were wicked and corrupt. They violated temple rules and showed contempt for God's sacred offerings. Samuel and Eli's sons were just three boys growing up in the temple, learning all the teachings to do their daily work. But the bible says that neither Samuel nor Eli's sons *knew* the Lord.

What does it mean to *know* someone? There is a huge difference between knowing someone and knowing about someone. A lot of people know about God or believe that God exists. However, our behavior does not change because we know about God or believe in God. Some studies suggest that as much as 97% of Americans acknowledge the existence of God in some way or another. However, you can watch the news, see all of the horrible things that go on in the world, all of the discrimination, all of the violence in our streets, all of the murders, the disregard for authority, the sexual sin that goes on all around us, and that would make us question how many people really know God.

To *know* means to be aware of, or to understand by personal experience. To *know* God means to personally relate to Him. Knowing God is having a personal relationship with Him. *Personal* means individual, special, intimate, not public, not like everybody else, but unique, mine, one-on-one, and one of a kind. *Relationship* means connection, bond, fitting together nicely, union. The bible's idea of *knowing* someone is relational, not just an intellectual exercise. It is more than just knowing information about someone. For instance, I know about the former First Lady of the United States, Michelle Obama. She is an amazing role model, beautiful, smart, and successful, but I would not say that I *know* her. To know her, I have to meet her and get to know her. We would have to reveal things to each other and be willing to share in each other's lives, which would eventually deepen our awareness and understanding of each other. Only through a personal relationship can you truly know a person.

God is deeply personal. In Amos 3:2, the Lord is speaking to the children of Israel and says *"You only have I known of all the families of the earth."* Does that mean God was not aware of other nations on the earth? Of course not. He knew about every nation. But He only *knows* Israel. He has a deep connection, a special bond, a personal relationship with His special people. God wants that same connection, a personal relationship with each and every one of us. God is personal. He is a person. God became flesh and lived among us here on earth, in the person of Jesus Christ. So now, through Christ, we can move past just knowing about God and really know God through a personal, one of a kind relationship with Him.

That is why Christianity is so unique. It is not a religion, it is a relationship with God through Christ Jesus, the Son. Jesus came down to earth and became a man to reveal who God is, not *what,* but who, and to reveal how we can have a personal relationship with Him. Jesus says, *"I am the way, the truth, and the life. No one can come to the Father except through me."* (John 14:6). Jesus is the way, the truth, and the life. Jesus is the way to know God, Jesus reveals the truth about who God is, and Jesus gives us the life of God. Think about that for a second, *the life of God*. We get to experience God's life. The life of God is real life. Unless you have the life of God, you do not have real life. Only God's life is life. Besides that, no other life can be counted as life because only the life of God is divine and eternal. The Greek word for "life" is *zoe*. Because the life of God is real life, whenever the New Testament in the original Greek speaks of this life, it always uses the word *zoe*, which refers to the highest life, eternal life.

"And this is eternal life", Jesus says, *"that they may know You, the only true God, and Jesus Christ whom You have sent."* (John 17:3). Here, Jesus defines what eternal life is. Eternal life is knowing God and Jesus Christ who was sent to make that possible. Eternal life is having an intimate awareness of God and personally understanding Him. If you want to experience eternal life, abundant life, Kingdom life, heaven on earth life, which is the life you deserve, then that life is only determined by our knowledge of God. Knowing God personally, relationally, from the heart through Christ, that is the purpose of your life. Holiness is a part of life. Evangelism and winning others to Christ are parts of life. Finishing school, landing a good job, raising a family, fulfilling our ministry call, being successful, are all parts of life, but none of that is the whole purpose of life. The purpose of life is to know God, personally for yourself. The purpose of life is to understand Him and know His ways, not His ways with somebody else, but His ways with you.

Psalm 103:7, says, *"He made known his ways to Moses, his acts to the children of Israel."* God did some great and mighty acts before the eyes of the Israelites. He parted the Red Sea, defeated the Egyptians, and brought them out of slavery. The people all saw those acts, but secretly, privately in a quiet place on the mountain, God made known His ways to Moses. You can see what a person does, but to know his ways, to know why he does them, and how he does them, and to know the way he is thinking when he does them, that is a deeper form of knowledge and that is how God wants us to know Him. How God was with Moses was for Him and Moses. How God is with you, with each one of us individually, now that is the exciting discovery!

My relationship with God knows no bounds. When I say God is with me, I do not mean in the traditional "churchy" sense. I mean God is literally with me wherever I go. We get up in the morning together, have coffee together, and we get dressed together. We talk all throughout the day. God gives me traffic tips as we ride in the car together. I ask His advice several times throughout the day. Before I send an email, go into a meeting, or answer my boss' questions, I ask God for wisdom. He helps me find my keys when I misplace them. I consult Him when I buy groceries or when I am deciding what to cook for dinner. When I am doing homework with my son, I ask God for all the answers. When I am disappointed, when I am afraid, when I am hurting, or when everything is just peachy, I share details of my day with God. He is an intricate part of my daily life.

To know God, you will need to have your own personal experiences with Him. If you have issues with your earthly father, you will get to know God as your Heavenly Father, *Abba*. If you are sick in your body, you will experience God for yourself as your healer, *Jehovah-Rapha*. If you are going through financial hardships, you will find out for yourself that God is your Provider, *Jehovah-Jireh*. You will know God as your Shepherd, *Jehovah-Rohi*. You will know Him as a Miracle Worker, *Jehovah-Nissi*. You will know God as Lord, *Adonai*. You will know God as your Peace, *Jehovah-Shalom*; and your Restorer, *Jehovah-Shammah*. He is *Elohim*, your Creator; *El Shaddai*, God Almighty; and *El Elyon*, God Most High. He is yours and yours alone. He is *your* eternal God, not like anyone else's. You will know Him for yourself!

Philippians 3:10 says, *"I want to know Christ—yes, to know the power of his resurrection and participation in his sufferings, becoming like him in his death, and so, somehow, attaining to the resurrection from the dead."* I want to know Christ. There's that phrase we have been talking about – *to know*. What God is saying in this passage is, "I want you to know me, understand me, all of me. I want you to know my suffering, so you will experience suffering. I want you to understand my death, so you will experience deadly conditions. But I also want you to know that because I resurrected from the dead, I have the power to raise you up and bring life to you! *Selah*.

God wants you to know that He has the power to bring life to you in any situation you face. In any circumstance that seems too hard to bear, any trial or test, He can deliver you. And you will know God's power and His strength when you have no more power or strength of your own, when you do not know what else to do, when you feel like you are dying because it hurts so bad. In those moments of desperation, you can run to God and experience the same power that raised Christ from the dead. Those experiences will cause you to declare for yourself that, "I know God!" These experiences will be yours alone to hold on to. No one else will be able to truly relate to those special times between just you and God. We all have to go to God for ourselves so that He can reveal Himself to us in a way that only we can truly receive it. It is really a personal thing.

Our difficulties are here for a reason. Our problems, challenges, weaknesses, and insecurities, are all here for a reason. You will have to know God in a way that is different from the way that I know Him. I will have to know God in a way that is different from the way that you know Him. We all have a personal path to walk. And when that path takes you through the valley of the shadow of death, you will not be afraid, because you will know God is with you. I do not care what it looks like, or what people say, you will declare and decree that, "I know God. I trust Him. He is my Comforter, He never leaves me nor forsakes me. He orders my steps and works all things together for my good. He is all powerful, He is faithful, and if He delivered me before, He will surely do It again!"

Will you pray like Moses? "Lord show me your glory; show me You, reveal yourself to me!" God will answer your prayer like He answered Moses' petition in Exodus 34:6, not with an earthquake or thunder bolts and lighting. He simply hides Moses in the cleft of a rock and – *"The Lord passed by before him, and proclaimed, The Lord, the Lord God, merciful and gracious, longsuffering, and abundant in goodness and truth, keeping mercy for thousands, forgiving iniquity and transgression..."*. God simply proclaimed who He was, His glory, what made Him

God, summed up in one word: LOVE! God is love (1 John 4:8). Ephesians 3:17-20 tells us that God wants us to be rooted and established in love and to grasp how wide and long and high and deep His love is. God wants you to know His love which surpasses knowledge—that you may be filled to the measure of all the fullness of Him. Being filled with God, maturing in the knowledge of Him and His love for you, fills you with His power. And God is able to do immeasurably more than all we can ask or imagine, according to His power that is at work within you.

When Moses got the revelation of God, the bible says Moses quickly fell to his knees and worshipped. You do not read Moses ever worshipping God up until this point. Because it takes a revelation of God, a vision of Him, to worship Him. The vision of God calmed all Moses' fears, removed every doubt, and he was ready to complete his assignment. A vision of God must be received in your spirit and become the source of everything you do! A vision of God reveals our inability and God's capability. A vision of God commands our surrender and so we willingly pray, "Lord, let your will be done." (Matthew 6:10).

You have to train to know God. Yes, you have a part to play in building this relationship. Getting to know God is a choice to train on Him, to learn about Him, and that positions you to receive a revelation from Him. Your training regimen must include spending time with God in prayer, talking with Him throughout the day. It should also include reading His Word every day. Training on God's Word means meditating on His Word and obeying what His Word says, which unlocks promising results for your life. Your training plan must also include spending time with other believers and submitting to leaders who will teach you, empower you, equip you, and encourage you. The right support system will help sharpen your skills, hold you accountable, develop your character, and help you to discover things about yourself that you did not see before.

When challenges arise, you apply what you have learned, you share your testimony, and help others through those very similar challenges. Training allows the Holy Spirit to reveal who God is to your heart. This knowledge will be sealed by your personal experiences with Him, which will cause you to know Him more intimately. You cannot know who you are until you know Who God is. Knowing God will change you over time. You will be transformed from glory to glory, growing closer and closer to the original reflection of God, the reflection you were created to be. Do you know who you were originally created to be?

CHAPTER FOUR

KNOW YOURSELF

If you have never read "The Five Love Languages" by Dr. Gary Chapman, you are seriously missing out on some keen insight that can transform your relationship for the better. In his book, Chapman explains that we tend to give and receive love in five main ways: words of affirmation, quality time, gifts, acts of service, and physical touch. While my husband's language is hands down physical touch and quality time, mine is no doubt - words of affirmation. For me, I beam when I hear how Chris thinks and feels about me. The words "I love you" warm my heart. But hearing *why* he loves me is heaven on earth. Conversely, rudeness, insults, and even a harsh tone can feel like torture. I am sure we all like a good compliment every now and then. But the reality is that we cannot get caught up in what people say to us or about us, whether positive or negative. Their words cannot be the basis for our identity, worth, or value. The only person we should be trusting with those things is God. Who does God say I am?

Many Christians struggle their whole lives to believe in their God-given identity. It is an identity crisis of mass proportions. Our Heavenly Father tells us the truth about Jesus and ourselves, while the devil constantly tells us lies. John 10:10 says that the thief (the devil) comes to steal, kill and destroy, but that Jesus came to give us "super abundant" life. So one of the devil's greatest tactics is to try and steal our greatest gift from God, the gift that is our identity as His beloved children. 1 John 3:1 says, *"See what great love the Father has lavished on us, that we should be called children of God!"*

Before Jesus started His public ministry, the Father proclaimed Jesus to be His beloved Son in Whom He was well pleased. Right after that, the devil's first words in tempting Jesus are, *"If You are the Son of God, tell this stone to become bread."* (Matthew 4:3). It is the same way the devil tempts us to doubt our identity today. He substitutes question marks for God's periods and often adds the word "*if*." But the Father, through Jesus, tells us who we are and this is confirmed by the Spirit.

Still, many of us still ask ourselves the age-old question: who am I?

In Mathew 16:13, Jesus poses two questions to His disciples: *"Who do people say that I am?"* and *"Who do you say that I am?"* These questions form the basis of identity. At one level, Jesus is checking the opinion polls to discover public perceptions of His person and His work. He does this, not because He needs the validation of people or to determine His next move. He does this as a set-up to His next more important question which will reveal whether His own disciples know Him. Jesus asks the disciples, "Who do people say that the Son of Man is?" They say some think He's John the Baptist, Elijah, Jeremiah, or one of the other prophets. Up to this point, Jesus has been attacked by the religious leaders of the day, His family thinks He is crazy, and others think He insults the God of Israel. Yet, He continues to draw large crowds and most have no clue of His true identity. Jesus does not care about what the people say about Him, but He does care about the understanding His disciples have of Him. Do they know who He is?

Jesus' disciples did life with Him for nearly three years. They watched Him live, heard Him speak, witnessed His miracles, observed His prayer life, and saw His courage in the face of opposition. The disciples knew a great deal about Jesus and witnessed His personal walk with the Father. Accordingly, it mattered deeply to Jesus, not what the masses thought about Him, but what James, John, Peter, and the others believed about Him. If Jesus' disciples were firmly planted in the truth of His identity, if they truly knew Him, then they would fulfill their assignment and the Kingdom of God would advance through them. They would essentially turn the world upside down (Acts 17:6).

In verse 15, Jesus asks the disciples, *"Who do you say I am?"* We do not know if there was a long pause, or if the disciples looked at each other with confused looks. We do know that Simon Peter answers, *"You are the Christ, the Son of the living God!"* Jesus replied, *"You are blessed, Simon son of John, because my Father in heaven has revealed this to you. You did not learn this from any human being."* Jesus was saying to Simon Peter, nothing on this earth has revealed this to you, no miracle that I worked, no logic that you have followed to reason it out, no sermon that was preached to you, no book you read. It was revealed to you by the Spirit. Peter received divine revelation of the true identity of Christ and he announced it to everyone that was listening. Here we see again the power of revelation.

Peter identified Jesus by stating His role as Christ the Messiah and His relationship, the Son of the Living God. In saying this, Peter revealed the true identity of Jesus. Jesus responds by blessing Peter and revealing Peter's true identity, *"Now I say to you that you are Peter (which means 'rock'), and upon this rock I will build my church, and all the powers of hell will not conquer it."* Peter's name means Rock. Rock is a metaphor to refer to someone or something as solid, hard, strong, and reliable. But when you read throughout the gospels, you do not see Peter exhibiting any of these rock-like qualities. The bible shows us that Peter was very much aware of his own sinfulness (Luke 5:8), often spoke out of turn (Mark 8:32-33; 9:5-6), and he denied knowing Jesus three times after bragging that he would ride or die for Jesus (Mark 14:29-31; 66-72).

Jesus names Peter "rock" not for his character, but for the revelation that Peter received about Jesus' identity. It was on that revelation, the rock, that Jesus would build His Church. Jesus named Peter, rock, because of the role Peter would fulfill as the leader of the Church. Jesus has placed this call, this role and purpose on Peter. In fulfilling this, Peter will know his true identity and purpose. In other words, a revelation of Christ unlocks the identity of yourself and your sphere.

Jesus saw who Peter was created to be long before Peter saw it in himself. If you asked Peter early on as a follower of Christ if he was going to be the leader of the Church, he would have told you to go on with that! If you were to tell me ten or even twenty years ago that I was going to be preaching the Gospel of Jesus Christ today, or even writing this book, I would not have believed it either. I would have told God that His plans were impossible and that I was not worthy. Have you ever looked at yourself and discredited God's plans for your life because you felt unqualified? The reality is, God does not call the qualified, He qualifies those who He calls. But we must allow Him the freedom to define our identity. Like Peter, when Jesus looks at us, He does not see what we are now, He sees what we can become if we embrace the truth of who we are in Him. He sees us in eternity, made in the image of God, predestined to do good works that He planned before the foundations of the world.

Many of us continue to ask that age-old question, who am I?

But that is not really the first question to ask yourself. The first question in life is, who is Jesus? This question continues to hang in the air even two thousand years later, and it is the question that one day every man and woman will be required to answer. Why? Because God *"...has set a day when he will judge the world with justice by the man he has appointed"* (Acts 17:31a). The true identity of Jesus Christ is a matter of life and death, both in regard to the quality of one's life now, and their future eternal destiny. When we recognize Jesus as Lord and Messiah, He will reveal to us the answer to the next question: "who am I?" We recognize who Jesus is and He in turn tells us who we are and the purpose for which we were created. Will you believe what He tells you?

Many times, words and wounds from people and our past cause us to believe that our identity is something other than what God calls us. We may have been called, or even called ourselves, failure, unlovable, not chosen, shameful or worthless. But God desires to give us a new name from His own mouth (Isaiah 62:2). Our God is in the name-changing business! All throughout scripture we see that God changes the names of His children to define their purpose despite what the person may look or act like in the moment. Because like Peter, when Jesus looks at us,

He sees past the brokenness, past the failures and fears, past the doubts and disappointments. It does not matter what people have said or done to you, how people may have labeled you, or how they may have condemned you. Your identity does not depend on something you do, have done, or what people say or think. Your true identity is who God says you are. He sees all that your future holds and is inviting you to live your most purposeful life yet in your true identity, an identity which is found in Christ Jesus.

So now the question has evolved from who am I, to who am I *in Christ*? Let me sum up for you the truth of God's Word concerning who you are in Christ. You are loved by God (1 John 3:3), created anew in Christ Jesus (2 Corinthians 5:17), complete in Him (Colossians 2:10). You are not a mistake (Psalms 139:16), you are His masterpiece (Ephesians 2:10), created in His image (Genesis 1:27). You are accepted (Ephesians 1:6), saved (Ephesians 2:8), and a citizen of Heaven (Philippians 3:20).

You are God's child (John 1:12), chosen and dearly loved (Colossians 3:12). You are royalty, holy, and God's special possession (1 Peter 2:9). You are a saint (Ephesians 1:1), blessed (Ephesians 1:3), and blameless (Ephesians 1:4). You are the temple of God (1 Corinthians 6:19), a member of Christ's body (1 Corinthians 12:27), and greatness is in you (1 John 4:4). You are forgiven (Colossians 1:14), set free (Romans 8:2), healed (Isaiah 53:5), an overcomer (Revelations 12:11), and more than a conqueror (Romans 8:37).

You are the head and not the tail, above and not beneath, the lender and not the borrower (Deuteronomy 28:12-13). You are alive with Christ (Ephesians 2:5) and are a partaker of His divine nature (2 Peter 1:3-4). Because of this, you are rooted, built up and strong (Colossians 2:7). You have no fear, but you have love, power, and a sound mind (2 Timothy 1:7). You are at peace with God, justified (Romans 5:1), and you are the righteousness of God (2 Corinthians 5:21). You are a new creation in Christ (2 Corinthians 5:17) and free from condemnation (Romans 8:1). You are redeemed (Colossians 1:14). In fact, you are redeemed from the curse of the law (Galatians 3:13) and from the hand of the enemy (Psalm 107:2).

You are the apple of God's eye (Psalm 17:8). You are dead to sin (Romans 6:11) for you have been crucified with Christ (Galatians 2:20) and are sealed with the Holy Spirit (Ephesians 1:13). You are the salt of the earth (Matthew 5:13) and the light of the world (Matthew 5:14). You are called by God, and He works everything out for your good (Romans 8:28). You are Christ's ambassador (2 Corinthians 5:20). And you must never forget that you are always in His thoughts (Psalm 139:17), because you are the adopted sons and daughters of Almighty God (Galatians 4:5).

I encourage you to train yourself on how God sees you. Your training regimen must include consistent meditation on scriptures that define who you are in Christ. Allow Jesus to shape your identity, pray that He would reveal the truth about who you are in His eyes. The more you train yourself and agree with God about your identity in Christ, the more your behavior will begin to reflect your God-designed destiny. Knowing who you are in Jesus is essential to your success in the sphere of service He has for you. Your understanding who you are in Christ will give you a strong foundation to dominate in your area of ministry and live the life you deserve.

CHAPTER FIVE

KNOW YOUR SPHERE

Finding and fulfilling your purpose is the greatest adventure you can have in this life. The journey to your purpose coincides with your lifelong journey of discovering God and who you are in Him. Knowing God and knowing who He calls you to be, guides you to the specific sphere of activity where you work to bring Him glory. *"For we are God's masterpiece. He has created us anew in Christ Jesus, so we can do the good things he planned for us long ago."* (Ephesians 2:10). God could have created everything imaginable and filled the earth Himself, but He chose to create mankind in His own image, to work alongside Him to manifest the earth's fullest potential. *"God blessed them, and God said to them, "Be fruitful and multiply, and fill the earth and subdue it; and have dominion..."* (Genesis 1:28). Through our work, God yields products, programs, and services, knowledge, information, and beauty, organizations, systems, and communities, growth, wealth and health, and praise, honor and glory to Himself.

Despite our sinful disobedience, which led us to lose our dominion in the earth, Jesus Christ came to earth to redeem man and to reclaim that had been lost in the Garden. *"For God was pleased to have all his fullness dwell in him, and through him to reconcile to himself all things, whether things on earth or things in heaven, by making peace through his blood, shed on the cross"* (Colossians 1:19-20). As we put our faith in the finished work of Christ, we become an extension of His work in the earth, the work of advancing the Kingdom of God. This is our purpose, this is the Great Commission, where Christ commands us to extend the reign of God over people's lives, making them disciples and teaching them to live as Christ the King commands.

The Gospel opens our eyes to the fact that we are God's chosen people, a royal priesthood, a holy nation, His special possession, called out of darkness into his wonderful light to declare His praises (1 Peter 2:9). And just as Christ could say to His Father at the end of His earthly assignment, *"I have glorified your name and finished the work you have given me to do,"* (John 17:4), likewise, when we finally fulfill our earthly assignment, we must be able to say to Christ, "We have glorified your name and have finished the work you gave us to do."

When God wants to influence a nation, He places servants in key areas of influence. A servant seeks to do the will of another. Moses was used to influence the nation of Egypt whose leader was Pharaoh. Daniel was used to influence Babylon whose leader was Nebuchadnezzar. Esther was used to influence Persia whose leader was Ahasuerus. In these examples, God's influence was advanced through His chosen servants in nations that were hostile to His people, so that His glory could be made to manifest.

God will catapult you to a place of influence and use you to be the extension of His Kingdom in the earth. The Kingdom of God is to expand, overtake, and overrule all the other false kingdoms of this world. That is why Jesus commands us to pray, "Thy Kingdom Come...on earth as it is in heaven." The Kingdom of God is to spread out like light, permeate like salt, and influence like yeast in dough.

In Os Hillman's book "Change Agent", he states: "If we are to impact any nation for Jesus Christ, then we will have to affect the seven spheres or mountains of society…These seven mountains are business, government, media, arts and entertainment, education, the family, and religion." Hillman goes on to say: "It is important to have conversions, but it is more important to have those who are converted operate at the tops of the cultural mountains from a biblical worldview." Everyone has a call and an assignment to one or more of these cultural spheres with the primary objective of advancing God's Kingdom.

For clarity, let me share some occupations that fall under the various spheres of influence:

- Business – Accountants, Budget Analyst, Managers, Economists, Human Resources Specialists, Tax Preparers, Entrepreneurs.

- Government – Judges, Court Reporters, Attorneys, Legal Secretaries, Politicians, Bureaucrats, Administrators, Law Enforcement, Military.

- Media – Writers, Advertisers, Broadcasters, Editors, Graphic Designers, Journalists, Marketers, Reporters, Photographers, Publishers, Translators, Researchers, Poets.

- Arts and Entertainment – Actors, Directors, Athletes, Dancers, Producers, Entertainers, Fine/Visual Artists, Musicians, Singers, Photographers, Fashion Designers.

- Education – Curators, Educational Staff, School Administrators, Librarians, Lecturers, Teachers, Teaching Assistants, Curriculum Developers.

- Family – Nanny, Husbands, Wives, Guardians, God Parents, Step Parents, Step Siblings, Parents, Grand Parents, Brothers, Sisters, Uncles, Aunties, Cousins.

- Religion – Intercessors, Non-Profit Ministers, Clergy, Pastors, Apostles, Teachers, Prophets, Evangelists, Missionaries, Church Administrators, Church staff.

If you find yourself in any of these occupations, then you have essentially identified your sphere of influence. There is no sphere more important than the other. All spheres must be permeated with God's influence through us, all spheres must work together to continue to bring God's Kingdom down to earth. We must declare Jesus' Lordship over all spheres of culture. Christ is:

- Jehovah-Jireh (Provider), Lord of business (Genesis 22:14)
- King of Kings, Lord of government (Revelation 17:14)
- Living Word, Lord of media (John 1:14)
- Creator, Lord of arts and entertainment (Isaiah 64:8)
- Teacher, Lord of education (John 13:13)
- Father, Lord of the family (1 John 3:1)
- High Priest, Lord of religion (Hebrews 4:14)

Revelations 5:12 says, *"Worthy is the lamb who was slaughtered to receive power, wealth, wisdom, strength, honor, glory, and praise!"* Power is the key to government. Wealth is the key to business. Wisdom is the key to education. Strength is the key to family. Honor is the key to religion. Glory is the key to arts and entertainment. Praise is the key to media. God's influence is mightier than any earthly influence. If we submit ourselves to God's will and yield to the leading of the Holy Spirit, we will effortlessly accomplish God's original assignment for us, to be fruitful, multiply, replenish, subdue, and take dominion. But we must do so in our specific sphere of influence.

We each have a God-assigned sphere of influence and we all have different people and situations that we are called to impact. However, many people try to operate outside of their God-assigned sphere. When you try to serve God in ways that you are not shaped to serve, it feels forced. When you try to overextend yourself outside of your God-assigned sphere you can negatively impact your growth and the growth of others. Operating outside or beyond your God-assigned sphere will produce limiting results and will frustrate your progress. It wastes your time, talent, and energy. Are you operating in your God-assigned sphere?

Let us examine the Apostle Paul. What made Paul so effective in life was that he knew his sphere. In 2 Corinthians chapter 10, the Apostle Paul is found defending his apostleship and authority against some haters and false teachers. They have come into the Corinthian church, which he started, trying to oppose and defame him. In verse 13, Paul says, *"We, however, will not boast beyond proper limits, but will confine our boasting to the sphere of service God himself has assigned to us, a sphere that also includes you. We are not going too far in our boasting, as would be the case if we had not come to you, for we did get as far as you with the gospel of Christ. Neither do we go beyond our limits by boasting of work done by others. Our hope is that, as your faith continues to grow, our sphere of activity among you will greatly expand."* (2 Corinthians 10:13-16).

Paul knew his sphere of service which was assigned to him by God. In Greek, the word "sphere" comes from the Greek word "kanon" which means "a boundary" or "place of activity" or "lane", like what runners would stay in as they raced. God had granted Paul a sphere of influence, a sphere of authority, and this sphere included the Corinthian church. Paul is declaring that he is not going outside of his lane, nor is he running in someone else's lane, but he is running in his own lane. Paul also knew that his sphere had limits and he was careful not to boast beyond those limits. He did not take credit for what God was doing in another's sphere of influence. He also did not overextend himself into an area God had assigned to another. However, Paul protected the sphere God assigned to him, the Corinthian church, like a shepherd would protect his sheep.

God gives all of us limits to our influence. Our authority has boundaries within the sphere to which God has appointed us. Your sphere of ministry has already been determined by God and you would be wise to accept this truth. He knew you before He formed you in your mother's womb. He predestined you to do good works that He planned long ago. You must accept the boundaries and limitations that God established for your life. You must be careful not to overextend yourself into a sphere not assigned to you, demanding to be heard, imposing your opinion, and forcing change. Remember, God has been using others to labor in the sphere way before you came into the revelation of your calling. Kingdom Essential: In ministry, God calls you, but people invite you. We cannot use our calling to invite ourselves in.

When we forget that God has established boundaries for our sphere of influence, one of the temptations we face is comparing ourselves to others. We can begin to compare the size of our ministry or business to that of others, we can compare our title to other people's titles. We can puff ourselves up in stature or beat ourselves up in discouragement. However, we each have a sphere of service with limits of influence which will differ from person to person. God is using others to advance the Kingdom and we should support one another and rejoice in the work of others that occupy our specific sphere. As hard as it may be, we cannot allow the spirit of competition to creep into what we are doing for the Kingdom of God. Our success is only measured by whether we are faithfully serving God in the work He has called us to do.

My sphere is business. God has called me to the business sphere. God has given me spiritual gifts of administration, teaching, faith, leadership, and prophesy to support leaders and their organizations. God certainly uses me in other spheres, like government and religion, but I have God-given authority in the business sphere here in my local geographic area and a bit wider now thanks to technology. By God's grace, I can operate effectively in my sphere of influence, using my talents, gifts, and unique experiences. God sends me clients that understand and yield to my God-given authority. My clients rely on my expertise as I teach, consult, and coach them in their professional endeavors. As my clients act by faith on my recommendations, we can expect to see positive results. However, if I try to operate outside of my sphere, if I step outside of my lane, out of my God-determined boundaries, the results can be negative and not just for me, but for others as well.

Your talents and gifts will work effortlessly in your sphere of influence. You attract the right people, platforms, and opportunities. In your sphere of influence your talents and gifts are cultivated and you begin to have a sense of fulfillment almost as if you are on assignment. Your talents and gifts can point to your assignment, but they may not necessarily *be* your assignment. Only God can give you clear direction on your assignment in the earth, but your assignment will always manifest within your God-assigned sphere of influence.

If God has not told you what your assignment is, then you should concentrate on developing and nurturing your talents and gifts until you are sure of your assignment. You should be serving in your church, volunteering in your community, taking classes, etc. If you have received your assignment, then you will note that your talents and gifts will always complement your assignment. God will couple your unique experiences with your talents and gifts to make you different from others who have also been called to your sphere of influence. So, you never have to worry about competing, comparing, or conning your way to destiny. What God has for you is for you, it is predestined and ordained to succeed. There is enough room in God's Kingdom for all His visionaries.

As a Kingdom Visionary, it is probably a safe bet that God has been releasing some fascinating visions about your life. A vision from the Lord creates an assignment from heaven. Vision is the beginning of finding your sphere of influence. In your sphere of influence is where you will accomplish your assignment from Heaven. As we discussed in the prior chapter, vision comes from God. The sooner you get connected to God and begin to position yourself to receive revelation from Him, the sooner He will lead you to your assigned sphere of influence. You must be able to discern when you receive a vision from God and then take decisive action.

There are three ways to know that you have a God-vision. First, visions from God are always scary. If your vision does not terrify you, then it is too small. It may be a good vision, but not a God-vision. A God-vision should be so huge that you are bound to fail unless God steps in. You should give the, "no way, for real, me!" response when you think about a God-vision. So, ask yourself, *how big is my vision*?

Second, a vision from God always requires other people. If your vision does not include others, then it is too narrow. Having a vision does not mean it is you against the world. A God-vision must include others. God will raise up a multitude to embrace and catch your vision. He will also raise up the people you are called to serve. When you rise, you raise others up with you. You do not have to know everything, God will send people strategically to help you birth the vision as well as people that need your vision. God is all about manifesting purpose in community!

Lastly, a God-vision always gets done! A vision without action is a daydream, but action without vision is a nightmare. Too many people talk about what they are going to do and never produce any results. But a God-vision always gets done and it produces fruit. It is not just talk, it is an agonizing thing in your belly that keeps you up at night and it pushes you to keep going. You take one step at a time toward accomplishing the vision that God has birthed in your heart. Vision produces forward action by faith. Faith without works is dead! Do you believe you have a God-vision in your heart? Then it should terrify you, it should involve others, and it gets accomplished!

Kingdom Essential: The most important part of implementing a vision God has given you is to first give it back to Him. Proverbs 3:5-6 says, *"Trust in the LORD with all your heart, and do not lean on your own understanding. In all your ways acknowledge*

Him, And He will make your paths straight." If you acknowledge God in the vision, which means turn the vision over to Him, grant Him access, and recognize Him in it, then He promises to give you the direction you need to succeed.

Kingdom Visionaries must know and dominate within their assigned sphere. God wants us to take our rightful place as heirs to His Kingdom and dominate in the specific area of ministry He predestined for us. Armed with revelation and faith, the life of a Kingdom Visionary will overflow in abundance and fullness as the Holy Spirit uses them to operate in the unique sphere for which they were created. God created us for a specific purpose and He expects us to make the most of what we have been given in the sphere that He designed for us. He does not want us to worry about or covet abilities or results of others. Instead, He wants us to focus on the talents, gifts, and experiences He has given us to use. Follow His original instructions, "Be fruitful, multiply, replenish, subdue, and take dominion." God said, *"I will make you into a great nation, and I will bless you; I will make your name great, and you will be a blessing."* That is a promise!

TRANSFORM

Holy Spirit, thank You for Your Word, thank You for enlightening Your people and for infusing us with Your wisdom. Thank You for giving us the mind of Christ. Help us to yield to Your leading to be transformed as You renew our minds. We stand on the truth of Your Word. Father, it is Your truth that is used to transform us through the power of the Holy Spirit. Manifest Your glory in the lives of Your people. Help us to seek You more and more. Help us to not just be hearers of Your Word, but doers of Your Word that we may experience real transformation. We will be transformed into the very image of our Lord and Savior Jesus Christ, that in Him we will overflow with power, faith, love, peace, joy, and favor. In Jesus' name. Amen.

CHAPTER SIX

THE BUSINESS OF CHANGE

American psychiatrist and author, Theodore Rubin, says, "The problem is not that there are problems. The problem is expecting otherwise and thinking that having problems is a problem."

Problems. Everyone has them, right? Think about it, every single person on this planet has been faced with some type of obstacle, issue, or difficulty. No matter how big or small, a problem is just that - a problem! It is something that is unwelcomed and can even be harmful, something that has to be dealt with or overcome. The opposite of a problem is a solution and the world has a ton of those to offer.

The world is obsessed with what I call the *Business of Change*.

The *Business of Change* fills bookstores, churches, and conference halls. It has made social media celebrities out of regular people and continues to fuel the pockets of self-help gurus around the world. Have you ever wondered why the self-help section in a bookstore is so massive? Take a stroll through your favorite bookstore and you will find the walls filled with huge selections of self-help books on topics like dieting and spirituality. It seems that whatever people are searching for tends to fit in the categories of personal growth, development, or transformation. People desire change. We live in a world where happiness is the end goal of almost every person's life. Everyone wants to be happy. Everybody is searching, hoping, and longing to find that "one thing" that will make them permanently happy. People want solutions to the plethora of problems they face on a daily basis in hopes of coming to even a remote state of happiness.

A few years ago, Oprah Winfrey packed out our local sports arena with her "Life You Want" Weekend. Thousands of women paid upwards of two hundred dollars to experience what they called a weekend of powerful transformation. Oprah promised that in this one weekend, not only would you see the possibilities of a new life, but it would be the life you want.

Oprah promised that each person at the conference would leave transformed, ready to take charge, and make it happen. Transformation, in just one weekend. The life you want, and *you* can make it happen. Wow! Where do I sign up? The hype and extravagance over this one weekend really caused me to think about transformation. Is it really *that* easy? Is transformation really like waving a magic wand and *poof* you are a new person with a whole new life, a problem-free life?

If transformation was really that easy, then, my God, I could just think of the possibilities. There would be an end to fretting over the right dress or the right pair of shoes. I could use my easy button and *poof*, transformation. No more diet and exercise. I would just use my easy button and *poof*, transformed to perfect health and just the right weight. Yeah, right! I *wish* it were that easy. Don't you? As hard as it is to change on the outside, just imagine how much harder it is to change on the inside. I contemplate all the struggles, challenges, and situations that I have gone through in my life, circumstances that I have experienced that have shaped me into the person I am today. I think about my weaknesses, my triggers, those areas in my soul that make my walk with Christ even more precious to me. And then I ask myself, *is transformation really that easy?*

Think about your own life, your personality, your nuances, what makes you tick. If you had a magic wand, an easy button, what would you change about yourself on the *inside* if you could? Would you change that:

- Impatient spirit, *"If you do not marry me now, it is over!"*
- Critical tongue that always has an opinion about everything, *"Ooooh girl, that color does not look right on you."*
- Envy, anger and resentment, *"I should've been the one to lead prayer, not her."*
- Ungrateful spirit, a spirit of entitlement, *"Uh, you're not going to fix me a plate?"*
- People pleasing spirit, an inability to say no? *"Honey, I have to go to prayer meeting tonight because Pastor needs me!"*
- Sexual temptation, *"But I love him!"*
- Financial mismanagement, *"I've just got to have this!"*
- Guilt? Shame? Pride? Arrogance?

The list can go on and on.

We all want to change something about ourselves. We all dream of being something different, a better version of the person we are today. We want change, we want answers, we want solutions. Advertisers know this. That is why you see countless ads promising that you can lose weight *now*, you can make money *now*, and you can get the life you want *now*!

The Business of Change is directed at people who want to change what they are and how they feel. This industry knows that when people wake up in the morning and look in the mirror, if all they see is the same old person staring back at them, another day older, deeper in debt, heavier, sicker, or lonelier than yesterday, then that reality, the reality they're seeing in the mirror, sparks a desire within them for change, for transformation, or for something different than their current reality. It can make a person want to move to another city, change jobs, get a facelift, buy a new car, start a new career, get a divorce, go to a new church, start working out, buy a new outfit, etc. Yet, will any these changes, result in real transformation?

All too often many of us will come face to face with our existence and feel like we are not thriving, but just merely surviving. In our search for answers, television personalities like Oprah, Ellen, Dr. Oz, Dr. Phil, and others, become our go-to source for enlightenment. These personalities make millions of dollars with promises of a new life in just one weekend or in just five simple steps. Now, do not get me wrong, I have read some great self-help books that have inspired me to transform. For example, *Eat the Cookie... Buy the Shoes* by Joyce Meyer inspired me to do a full head-to-toe makeover for my 35th birthday.

I am super structured and over the years of working in bureaucratic bliss as a government analyst, my wardrobe suffered. I got tired of the "you look old" comments from my family and decided to go all out. When I walked into church after not having seen anyone for a full week, they could hardly recognize me. My hair, usually in a neat Condoleezza Rice bob, had been transformed into a Beyoncé weave of wavy curls flowing down my back! My clothes, usually black, grey, or brown in color, had been transformed into red, hot pink, and blue. With full make-up and accessories, I was determined to garner a WOW factor to shut up the critics. And that, I did. My social media page was buzzing at record highs with compliments and OMG's. The transformation was dramatic. I looked like a different person and all it took was a few hours of make-up, colored clothes, and some hair extensions.

If only spiritual transformation were that easy. Just read a book, see a counselor, attend a conference, pinky promise to God to be different, make a resolution, shed a few tears at an altar, memorize a few verses, and BOOM, just like that, total transformation into a mature, godly Christian experiencing abundant life. I'll be honest with you, it is not easy. I have gone through seasons of my life where I have felt like I was in a Christian rat-race. I felt miserable. Life seemed boring and pointless. I know I am not alone. Some of you are in search of a quick fix, *anything* that will be effective and preferably pain-free to get you to the abundant life Jesus promised. If only God, or someone else, would do something *to* us so that we could experience a once-and-for-all victory so that we would not have to keep wrestling with the same old problems and issues.

I am here to tell you that there is no quick fix. One weekend, one revival, or one book will not produce real transformation. Kingdom Visionaries need a kingdom strategy for transformation. Ephesians 4:15 says, *"...but speaking the truth in love, we are to grow up in all aspects into Him who is the head, even Christ,"*. Truth be told, we must grow up to live a victorious Christian life. To grow up means to develop, to evolve, and that takes time.

As a child of God, you must come to grips with the truth that our

Heavenly Father has given us one road, one plan, one way to attain real transformation. It is part of His strategic plan to bring us into the life we deserve and were predestined to live. God's process to real transformation is the solution to all of life's problems. It will result in the life we truly want here on earth and in eternal life with God in Heaven. But first, we must understand what real transformation is.

CHAPTER SEVEN

REAL TRANSFORMATION

The Bible says that in order for us to experience transformation, we have to renew our minds. Before anything can truly and deeply change in us, our minds must first be changed. Romans 12:2 reads, *"Do not conform to the pattern of this world, but be transformed by the renewing of your mind. Then you will be able to test and approve what God's will is—his good, pleasing and perfect will."* Be transformed by the renewing of your mind, what is the Apostle Paul talking about?

Paul was very intentional in how he wrote the book of Romans. The Book of Romans is touted by Christian scholars as *"Paul's Masterpiece."* Paul was able to summarize the entire Christian faith into one book. In the book of Romans, Paul not only introduces himself to the believers in Rome, but he maps out the whole Gospel story in one book. He details God's plan for believers and how we are saved by grace, through faith in Jesus Christ. Then he tells us how to live in response to the Gospel.

In the first eleven chapters, the Apostle Paul breaks down the Gospel so effectively, that immediately in chapter twelve he begins to exhort us on how we are to live in response to God's mercy toward us. He says in chapter 12 verse 1, *"Therefore, I urge you, brothers and sisters, in view of God's mercy, to offer your bodies as a living sacrifice, holy and pleasing to God—this is your true and proper worship."*

The word *therefore* in this verse means this chapter is built on something that has already been discussed in chapters one through eleven. Paul summarizes the totality of everything he wrote in these preceding chapters and calls it *"God's mercy"*. And what an amazing summary it is! Paul says, in view of God's mercy, in other words:

- because of the free gift of grace and favor of God that has come to you through Jesus Christ,
- in view of the fact that Christ paid the penalty that you deserved,

- in light of the fact that He chose you, called you, justified you, and will glorify you, and
- that He is for you, and nothing will ever separate you from His love.

In view of all these mercies, you should *therefore* give your whole lives in service to God as living sacrifices. Think about your life at this day and time. Are you living in service to God? Are you living a sacrificial life?

Paul says living a sacrificial life is what it means to worship God. Worship is more than coming to church once a week on Sunday, but rather, it is the offering of your whole life to God. It is a <u>lifelong, every day</u>, in <u>every way</u> offering unto God <u>everything</u> that makes up your life. It is your time, your talents, your treasures, your career, your children, your home, your relationships, your heart, body, mind and soul. It is <u>everything</u> offered sacrificially to God in service to Him. This is our reasonable worship of the Lord after all the mercies He has lavished on us. So, Paul then says in verse 2, do not conform – but be transformed.

The offering of our whole lives to God, which is our true and proper worship unto God, requires transformation. It is a sacrificial undertaking, which means it is going to cost you big! You must surrender all of your possessions, goals, dreams, desires, your very identity, releasing control of your own life to your Creator. In order for us to surrender, it means that we must deny ourselves and relinquish things like needing to be in charge, needing to have all the answers in advance, or needing to look good or to be famous. It means walking with God, often into the unknown. It means trusting Him to lead and provide.

If we are to present our bodies as living sacrifices, holy and pleasing to God, then we have to surrender, die to our flesh daily and yield to His will. That is real worship. Real worship requires complete non-conformity to the world, its systems, its way of thinking. Jesus says in Matthew 16:24-25, *"If anyone would come after Me, let him deny himself and take up his cross and follow Me. For whoever would save his life will lose it, but whoever loses his life for My sake will find it."* Are you ready to surrender you whole life to God?

When I think about surrendering or submitting to any authority, I am forced to think about my weakness. Oh, how I hate feeling weak or being reminded of my weaknesses. I worked so hard to be the best in school, to get a good job, to marry by a certain age, to please people, and be popular, but I was never satisfied or happy. I can almost bet that if you did some searching, you, too, would find the same distain for feeling weak. I strived to epitomize the world's standard of what constituted real strength, but I have come to know that God's measure for strength is strictly associated with our total dependence on Him. Instead of looking for strong, independent people, God seeks those who know they are actually weak and inadequate. God will take us through a process to face and embrace our weaknesses and inadequacies in order to get us to a place of complete dependence on Him.

Let us just take a moment and think about the situations you are faced with at work, at home, or even in church. Are you depending on Christ for wisdom, courage, and strength? Or are you relying on yourself? Living a surrendered life means you depend on Christ, presenting your body as a living sacrifice. If you find yourself relying on yourself, then you are walking in pride. When you live in pride you have simply closed your eyes to the reality of your condition, a condition we all have.

We were all born into sin and shaped in iniquity (Psalm 51:5). We are predisposed to disobey God and to be selfish. Because of our sinful nature, we are weak and it is impossible for us, in our own strength, to resist the devil and to be holy and pleasing to God. Roman 8:7-8 says, *"For the sinful nature is always hostile to God. It never did obey God's laws, and it never will. That's why those who are still under the control of their sinful nature can never please God."*

The world's definition of transformation must also be rejected. The world says personal success is transformation. The world says transformation is the ability to achieve your own goals. The world says transformation is the ability to control your own life, be branded, well-liked, or to enhance yourself in some form or fashion. This kind of false transformation is what the world constantly offers as real change, but it is misleading. You see, Oprah's Life You Want Weekend may be fun and exciting, but fun and excitement fades. When you get home from that conference, and are face to face with your reality, nothing the world is selling you will result in real transformation. Because *"… the wisdom of this world is foolishness with God."* (1 Corinthians 3:19). In other words, the wisdom of the world is only valuable when it humbly bows to the wisdom of God. But in our flesh, we look to rock-stars, pop idols, self-help gurus, or religious moguls for wisdom, putting all of our confidence in the flesh and not in our Creator.

We were created to be like our Creator. God Himself is holy and He wants His people to be holy as well (Peter 1:15-16). So, Paul says, do not conform to this world with its superficial values and customs, but be transformed. The Greek word for *transformed* in Romans 12:2 is related to the English word metamorphosis. When you think of metamorphosis you think of a caterpillar transforming into a butterfly. It is a gradual change that happens on the inside and produces a total transformation on the outside. Paul says to be transformed is to experience a progressive change from one thing to another. When the caterpillar changes into a butterfly it becomes what God always intended it to be. Accordingly, real transformation will ultimately reveal who God originally created us to be. But who were we originally created to be?

From the very beginning, God's plan has been to make us like His Son, Jesus Christ. God announced this plan at creation: *"And God said, Let us make man in our image, after our likeness."* (Genesis 1:26). But our image has been damaged and distorted by sin. However, the Good News is that God sent Jesus to the world to be our example in all things and to die on the cross to restore the full image we had lost. But that does not stop the devil from blinding people's heart from the truth of the gospel of the glory of Christ who is the image of God (2 Corinthians 4:4). We need to combat the spiritual identity crisis in the Body of Christ in order for real transformation to be manifested in God's people.

2 Corinthians 3:16-18 tells us, *"Nevertheless when one turns to the Lord, the veil is taken away. Now the Lord is the Spirit; and where the Spirit of the Lord is, there is liberty. But we all, with unveiled face, beholding as in a mirror the glory of the Lord, are being transformed into the same image from glory to glory, just as by the Spirit of the Lord."* God knew that when you turned to Him, all you knew were the things of this world. He knew that you thought like the world, acted like the world, and settled for what the world had to offer you. Even so, that did not change the truth that the veil was removed from your heart when you turned to Him. The veil that once blocked and prohibited you from discerning spiritual things, that veil of ignorance, the veil of unbelief, the veil of self-righteousness and pride. The veil that once blocked your ability to get a revelation of the truth of God's Word is now gone.

Now, with an unveiled face, we can sense the Spirit of the Lord. And where the Spirit of the Lord is, there is liberty! There is freedom to explore, to learn, to experience the endless possibilities of a relationship with an eternal God. There are no more limits or boundaries. And as we continue to behold, as in a mirror, the glory of the Lord, we are being transformed into the same image of Him, from glory to glory. Colossians 1:15 declares that Christ is the image of the invisible God. So real transformation means we are all being transformed into the very image of Jesus Christ.

With the veil lifted from your heart you can behold the glory of God as in a mirror. The Word of God is described as a mirror. James 1:22 reads, *"Do not merely listen to the word, and so deceive yourselves. Do what it says. Anyone who listens to the word but does not do what it says is like a man who looks at his face in a mirror and, after looking at himself, goes away and immediately forgets what he looks like. But whoever looks intently into the perfect law that gives freedom, and continues in it—not forgetting what they have heard, but doing it—they will be blessed in what they do."*

The Bible is a mirror and like the mirrors in our homes it helps us to evaluate ourselves. You look at a mirror and decide if you need to make any changes before you leave out for the day. So is the purpose of the Word of God for us. We must look intently into the Word, behold it, seek it, study it, and meditate on it. It is not a momentary glance. As you behold it, you must then do what it says. You must obey the Word. Obedience is one of the foundational virtues that Jesus forms in the lives of His disciples. He gives us the strength to obey as we make the decision to obey. Obedience is the cornerstone of our worship and one of the chief ways we demonstrate our love for God (John 14:15).

However, if all you do is look in the mirror, but you do not make a decision to adjust yourself, then you are deceiving yourself. For example, if I look in the mirror and see that my shirt is on backwards, but I choose to walk out of the house and do not turn it around the right way, then I am deceiving myself. My shirt is in fact on backwards and now everyone will know it. The same would hold true in my spiritual life. Regardless of my church attendance, the number of scriptures I memorize, or how gifted I am in administration, if I fail to evaluate myself based on my mirror, aka the Word of God, and decide to take corrective action, then my transformation is stunted.

We must not just be hearers of the Word, but also doers of the Word. Being a doer of God's Word opens the door for the Holy Spirit to transform you by the renewing of your mind. You have got to renew your mind in order to see real transformation in your life. Renewing your mind means that instead of applying the world's lies to your life, you apply God's truth to your life. If we do not renew our minds, we will be hoodwinked by the father of lies, the devil. But our Heavenly Father does not deceive! He wants you to know His will for you. His will is good, pleasing, and perfect.

When people ask, "What is God's will for my life?", what they are really asking is, "What does God want me to do with my life?" Well, there is no trick to knowing God's will. His will is in His Word. No doubt that God has a plan for our lives (Jeremiah 29:11), as well as *good works* which He prepared beforehand for us to do (Ephesians 2:10). But God's will for us is clearly noted in 1st Thessalonians 4:3, *"For this is the will of God, your sanctification"*. Are you ready for real transformation?

The process of transformation is called sanctification. Sanctification is the progressive transformative work of the Holy Spirit in a believer's life following their salvation. It is God's way of making us His special possession in Christ, setting us apart to fulfill His purpose for us. Sanctification is God's will for you (1 Corinthians 1:30). God's will is to see you transformed into the likeness of Jesus. God cares more about who we are becoming, than what we are doing.

We are to stand out in this world. We are to become different people with different values, different attitudes, different motivations, different thoughts, different words, and different actions. As we go through this process, we become progressively freed from sin and more and more under the Spirit's control. When we are submitted to the process of sanctification, we are more fully alive, becoming all that God predestined for us to be. We will, therefore, start walking through life in-step with God and His will. When we focus on God's desire to transform us, He teaches us how to lay hold of the life we deserve, abundant life.

Some of you may be ready for real transformation to manifest in your lives and others may still be holding out for the quick fix to glory. But guess what? You can save all the money you spend on self-help gurus because transformation, aka sanctification, is a non-negotiable requirement for every believer! Transformation is absolutely necessary. It must and will happen. You do not have an option – you must be transformed! If there is no transformation, then there is no salvation. Have you truly turned to the Lord? If so, then you must transform. Romans 8:29 says, *"For whom he did foreknow, he also did predestinate to be conformed to the image of his Son, that he might be the firstborn among many brethren."* This verse says, all believers have been predestined, not just to be saved, but to be conformed to the image of Jesus.

Transformation is a must for every born-again believer. So, if you have been chosen to be saved and chosen to go to heaven, then you have also been chosen and called to be conformed to the image of the Son! You are being transformed to love like Him, transformed to go from living a life of fear to living a life of faith. You are being transformed to live in God's presence, to carry His glory, to have peace that surpasses all understanding, and to glorify God through good works. You are being transformed to a life of purpose, transformed to be like your big brother, Jesus. But you must renew your mind.

CHAPTER EIGHT

RENEWING YOUR MIND

When I rededicated my life to Christ in 2009, I started attending church regularly and making new friends, but I was still struggling with unforgiveness. God moved mightily in my life in the short time since joining Soul Harvest Creative Praise Ministries, but I knew He was not finished. I needed to revisit my past and face the many hurts and pains, and even my own mistakes. God would not have it any other way.

I heard His still small voice say, "It is time to forgive." At that point in my life, I no longer had the answers. I was not turning back. I wanted everything God had for me. The abundant life Jesus died to give me depended on me forgiving my rapist, my father, many others, and most importantly – myself. After I released the offenses and offenders to God, I was finally ready for Jesus to take the reins of my life and lead me down the unknown narrow road of transformation.

I shared that very private part of my life to say this, real transformation begins when we surrender our will and allow Jesus to completely invade the darkness in our souls. When Jesus says, *"I am the light of the world"* (John 8:12), He is letting us know that everything we are trying to hide from others and from God will be exposed in His presence. Many times, we try to avoid God because when we get close to Him we step into His light and sometimes we are not quite ready to be fully exposed and get rid of our darkness. We keep our sins hidden in the dark, allowing fear, rebellion, or pride to rule our lives and real transformation to elude us.

However, God will not leave us to sit and die in our pain. Jesus came to give us life, and life more abundantly. He paid the price for us to have this life. The redemptive work of the cross is already finished. Now it is time to embark on the process of transformation. As I poured into the scriptures, wrestling with God all along the way, I read account after account of God's transformational power. I read, obeyed, and believed wholeheartedly that God would change me from a bitter, rejected, and wounded woman, to a joyful, free, and healed daughter of the King. I was ready to be used by God for whatever purpose I was predestined for. And He delivered what He promised. A renewed mind.

Many still struggle with temptations in their mind, bitterness, depression, fear, hopelessness, frustrations, negativity, and down-right evil thoughts. There is a constant battle that rages in the mind. But, there is a way to begin to end this struggle! 2 Peter 1:3-4 says, *"His divine power has given us everything we need for life and godliness through our knowledge of him who called us by his own glory and goodness. Through these he has given us his very great and precious promises, so that through them you may participate in the divine nature and escape the corruption in the world caused by evil desires"*.

Everything we need for life and godliness comes through the knowledge of Christ. Life and godliness are a direct result of knowing God and His will for your life. That is why Paul said to be transformed by the renewing of your mind. In other words, through the continuous renewing of your mind with the knowledge of His Word and applying the Word of God to your life, we are able to escape the corruption in the world because we become transformed to participate in the divine nature of God!

Transformation is not automatic, it is a process. It is a process of becoming what you already are. Because of the finished work of Jesus Christ on the cross, you are justified, meaning you are declared righteous in the eyes of God. 2 Corinthians 5:17 says that in Christ we are a new creation. The old is gone the new has come. 1 Peter 1:23 says it like this – *"having been born again, not of corruptible seed but incorruptible, through the word of God which lives and abides forever."* After we are born again, however, we still look the same on the outside. We still think the same even though God said we are new creations, completely different and changed on the inside, in the spirit. How do we bridge the gap?

We have got to renew our minds. We must renew our minds to everything God's Word says we are. In doing so, God will transform our lives into the new creation that we are. We will transform and exhibit God's nature, character, and attributes through our continuous knowledge and understanding of Him. Knowing and understanding His Word is what brings about our transformation, and thereby our freedom. Jesus said it like this in John 8:31-32, *"If you abide in my Word, then you are My disciples indeed. And you shall know the truth, and the truth shall make you free."*

Nothing can change the lives of people like the Word of God. An alcoholic or addict can be transformed to live sober and clean lives just by starting to read the bible. A selfish, self-centered, abusive husband can be transformed into a humble, God-honoring servant that loves his wife as Christ loved the church because he started reading the bible. Many Christians focus on the sad state of affairs of the laws of our country and try to change them to fit our faith. However, laws have never been able to change the human heart.

God's law is holy, just, and good (Romans 7:12). However, because of our sinful nature, we cannot keep God's law. The law made nothing perfect (Hebrew 7:19) because it could not change any human heart. You can make laws to outlaw racism, but no law will turn a bigot into a lover of people of diverse races. Only God can do that. We have seen the power of God over the hearts of man. He had the power to harden Pharaohs' heart in Exodus, but God also gives man a heart to know Him (Jeremiah 24:7).

Colossians 3:1-43 declares, *"... you were raised with Christ, so seek those things which are above, where Christ is, sitting at the right hand of God. Set your mind on things above, not on things on the earth. For you died, and your life is hidden with Christ in God. When Christ who is our life appears, then you also will appear with Him in glory."* This scripture teaches us that our real life is hidden in Christ, so we are to set our minds on Him and on Heaven where He is. You do not have to worry about what God wants you to do with your life, because when Christ becomes apparent in you, when the fruit of His Spirit is seen in your life, then the *real* you will appear with Him in all glory! So, who is the *real* you?

The question of "Who is the real me?" is always an interesting one. Am I the bossy, moody, and dictatorial me? Or am I the me who stops to chat, gives you my last, and is a quintessential hugger? Our two natures, flesh and spirit, are in constant war against each other. But one is the *real* you and the other an impostor. God does not want you focusing on who you used to be. *"For you died, and your life is now hidden with Christ in God."* (Colossians 3:3). The old you is gone, killed with Christ on the cross and buried with Him. Even though sometimes it may feel like the rude and thoughtless person is the real you, the truth is that our new identity is in Christ, in God. Although it may not look like it, our real self is to be found with Him. But you must renew your mind to that truth.

If we can get the truth of Romans 12:2, to be transformed by the renewing of our minds, it will answer the question of how we grow as believers and how we experience abundant life in Christ. If we apply this truth to our lives, in time we will see that our worship will never be the same. It will transform from a self-centered worship to a God-centered worship. Our love will never be the same, it will transform from a conditional love of a select few to a genuine unconditional love of others born out of deep concern and compassion. We will not even look at ministry the same way. Our view will transform from a burdensome task-driven volunteer job to the forceful advancement of the Kingdom of God! It is through the process of renewing our minds by which Christians both transform into the very image of Christ and transition into the life we were predestined to live.

CHAPTER NINE

TRAINING PLAN

Real transformation can only happen by the Holy Spirit. You heard me right; you cannot transform yourself. None of us can overcome our sins and weaknesses without God's help. God makes that help available to us through His Holy Spirit. *"For if you live according to the flesh you will die; but if by the Spirit you put to death the deeds of the body, you will live. For as many as are led by the Spirit of God, these are the sons of God"* (Romans 8:13-14). We cannot do any of this in our own strength. On our own strength, we cannot give our bodies as a living sacrifice. We cannot keep ourselves from becoming conformed to this world's system. You must stop falling into the trap of thinking that if you just try harder, you will get better.

For many believers, the transformation experience is described as a constant cycle of commitment, failure, and confession. Then re-commitment, fail again, and confess again. Then re-commit, fail again, and then give up. That is because trying harder generally sets us up for failure. Paul says, "be transformed," he does not say, "transform yourself," because that would be impossible. We do not have the power to change our depraved mind into the mind of Christ. Only God can do that for us. We must be transformed by the Spirit of God. While I am not here to tell you to keep trying to be different, you do have a part to play in the process. The work of renewing our minds is God's work, and ultimately, He alone will do it. But He does call us to cooperate with Him by disciplining ourselves so that the transformation can actually take place.

1 Corinthians 9:25 says, *"Everyone who competes in the games goes into strict training. They do it to get a crown that will not last; but we do it to get a crown that will last forever."* The reason many people give up on transformation or they reach a certain point and do not desire to go any higher in God is because we drive ourselves crazy *trying* to be transformed when the bible calls us to train to be transformed. There is a huge difference between trying to do something and training to do it. Take for example a marathon. How many of us could run a

marathon right now? Many of us could not fathom it, even if we tried, really, really hard. But many of us could run a marathon eventually, if we instead trained for it. Transformation always involves training, not just trying. What do you train with?

Well, athletes train with weights. Children of God train with the Word. 2 Timothy 3:16-17 says, "*all Scripture is God-breathed and is useful for teaching, rebuking, correcting and training in righteousness, so that the man of God may be thoroughly equipped for every good work*". It is the Word that equips us and prepares us for this life. We have to go into training to get ourselves in position so that the Holy Spirit can do what only He can do – renew our minds.

In Part 1 of this book, I shared three specific areas that you must train in to achieve the abundant life you deserve: God, self, and sphere. These are our strategic priorities. In strategic planning, strategic priorities are the areas of focus that determine how an organization brings their vision to reality. By now, you should have an understanding of God's ultimate vision for you – *transform into the image of Christ*. You should also be able identify any major gaps between this vision and your current reality.

Does your relationship with God need to expand? Are you receiving revelation from God? Are you still dealing with identity issues, low self-esteem, self-image issues? Are you questioning your purpose or wondering how to go to the next level? Your training plan should have goals that target growth in the areas of God, self, and sphere. By making progress in these areas and being faithful to the vision, we should expect to see transformation manifest in our lives.

With God's Word as our foundation, focus, and filter, we must develop specific goals to help us achieve God's vision for our lives. At the end of this book, I have included a worksheet to help you develop your own strategic training plan. To illustrate this approach, I'd like to share the training plan I initiated when I got saved and the corresponding scriptures which I meditated on to renew my mind in the strategic priority of knowing God:

GOAL 1: ACCEPTANCE: I must accept the fact that only the Holy Spirit can bring renewal. Only the Spirit can cause me to be illuminated within and convinced of truth.

- 1 Corinthians 2:14: "The man without the Spirit does not accept the things that come from the Spirit of God, for they are foolishness to him, and he cannot understand them, because they are spiritually discerned."

- In Ephesians 1:17-18: "I keep asking that the God of our Lord Jesus Christ, the glorious Father, may give you the Spirit of wisdom and revelation, so that you may know him better. I pray that the eyes of your heart may be enlightened in order that you may know the hope to which he has called you, the riches of his glorious inheritance in his holy people."

GOAL 2: PRAY: I must ask God for a hunger and a desire for His Word and for wisdom to understand it.

- James 1:5: "If any of you lacks wisdom, you should ask God, who gives generously to all without finding fault, and it will be given to you."

GOAL 3: FILL MY DAY WITH THE WORD: If I get the Word into my mind, God will get the Word into my heart.

- Colossians 3:16: "Let the message of Christ dwell among you richly as you teach and admonish one another with all wisdom through psalms, hymns, and songs from the Spirit, singing to God with gratitude in your hearts."
- Romans 10:17: "So then faith comes by hearing, and hearing by the word of God."

- Joshua 1:8: "Keep this Book of the Law always on your lips; meditate on it day and night, so that you may be careful to do everything written in it. Then you will be prosperous and successful."

a) Attend church service and bible study weekly.

b) Change my music, TV shows, and fill my time with church activities.

c) Google the Word for answers to questions and guidance for areas of weakness.

d) Include scripture in my prayers and develop a prayer schedule.

NOTE: I had to meditate on the word, which is not something that can be taught. In Hebrew, to meditate means to moan, utter, speak. Meditation is not a technique, but it is an act born out of a love and a delight in His Word.

e) Change my company and begin hanging out with people who build me up in Christ.

Kingdom Essential: We need to be connected to a community of believers who will reinforce the reality of God's Kingdom. We will eventually become like the people we hang out with. Do not allow yourself to be distracted from the things of God by aligning yourself with people who are not like minded.

GOAL 4: CONTROL MY THOUGHTS. Do not feed on thoughts that contradict God's Word. I have the ability to decide what I will concentrate on.

- 2 Corinthians 10:3-6 says, "For though we walk in the flesh, we do not war according to the flesh. For the weapons of our warfare are not carnal but mighty in God for pulling down strongholds, casting down arguments and every high thing that exalts itself against the knowledge of God, bringing every thought into captivity to the obedience of Christ."

Kingdom Essential: Stop dwelling on negative, condemning thoughts. Every time you meditate on a negative, condemning thought like low self-esteem, failure, or lack, you are making them stronger! The more you mediate on thoughts of victory, the victor in you grows stronger and the victim mentality grows weaker and weaker. Philippians 4:8 tell us to, *"meditate on whatever things are true, whatever things are noble, whatever things are just, whatever things are pure, whatever things are lovely, whatever things are of good report, if there is any virtue and if there is anything praiseworthy—meditate on these things."*

Dietitians say, "You are what you eat" and that is true physically. But that is also true mentally and spiritually. Matthew 4:4 tells us, *"man shall not live off bread alone, but by every Word that proceeds out of the mouth of God."* When people are dieting, they only eat and drink certain things. If you offer them chips, candy, or soda, they may say, "No thank you, that's not on my eating program." Why? Because they are on a strict diet. We need to take this same approach as it relates to our transformation. Stop eating mental junk food that is polluting your mind. Thoughts that contradict God's Word over your life are mental junk foods that are polluting your mind.

When those thoughts come to you saying, "you're never going to be happy" or "you're never going to accomplish your dreams", *do not* focus on them. Do not dwell on what you think are impossibilities in your life. Do not dwell on those people who have hurt you or even your past mistakes. Are you easily offended? Do you fear rejection of others? Are you in bondage to what others think about you? Then you must renew your mind!

You are not who people say you are. You are who God says you are. When those thoughts come, turn them around by declaring what God says about you. God says you are a masterpiece, talented, creative, strong, confident, and disciplined. You are an overcomer, more than a conqueror, and able to do all things through Christ. You will fulfill every God-given dream in your heart because the Almighty God favors you. God says your latter days will be greater. God says you are anointed, blessed going out and blessed coming in, and that everything you put your hands to prospers and succeeds (Deuteronomy 28:1-14).

Develop your training plan using the infallible Word of God and in time you will become persuaded of truth. I am persuaded of who I am in Christ. I am persuaded of where I am going. I am confident that God is in control of every detail of my life, that nothing happens by accident, and that all things are working together for my good.

With a renewed mind, you will be able to do exactly what the Apostle Paul says, *"test and approve what God's will is—his good, pleasing and perfect will."* God's will for you is what's best for you and brings you the greatest satisfaction, freedom, and joy. Living out your purpose, there is nothing better, nothing more pleasing, and nothing more perfect. Decide to go into training today. Commit to this lifelong process of transformation by the renewing of your mind and become all that God predestined for you to be from glory to glory.

TRANSITION

Father, I thank You for what You have done, what You are doing, and for what You will do. Lord, I perceive that we are in an intense season where something is shifting in the spiritual realm. I ask now, that You speak to the hearts of Your people. Speak particularly to those who feel like they do not know what their next step is. Holy Spirit, I pray for every Kingdom Visionary, every marketplace leader, and all the faithful forerunners in the Body of Christ. My prayer is that You make their ears to hear one word very clearly in this season, and that word is transition. May they take heed to Your still small voice and step out into the deep of Your glory to experience the life You predestined for them to enjoy. Thank You for this season of transition. In Jesus' name. Amen.

CHAPTER TEN

THE COURAGE ZONE

When I graduated college and moved from my hometown of Miami, away from all of my family, to the City of Atlanta where I did not know anyone, I was scared. Yes, I was excited too, but this was completely outside of my comfort zone. Looking back, I really had nothing going for me in Miami. College was over, friends and family were living their own lives. I had bills to pay and a great sense of needing to accomplish something great with my life. The employment prospects were dismal and no doors were opening for me at home. That was my life until I saw an ad for a Human Resources position in Atlanta. Then my spirit leaped.

I was nervous yes, but at that very moment, I knew this was an opportunity to do something big. I had to make a decision. Do I stay here at home and figure it out with what I know? Or do I move forward, apply for the job and take a chance with the unknown? In that moment fear reared its ugly head and soon thereafter doubt began to whisper in my ear hoping to take root in my heart. Had I allowed fear to grip me and hold me hostage to the life I knew, instead of taking a chance on the opportunities afforded to me in something or someplace new, I may not be where I am in my career today. Praise God for transition.

As I found out then and several more times throughout many other transitions over the years, no aspiration can ever be accomplished from within your comfort zone. Kingdom visions are just too big for comfort zones. Instead of a comfort zone, Kingdom Visionaries ought to get used to operating from more of a "courage zone". Because we can never hope to achieve success unless we are willing to embrace change, deal with the discomfort of taking risks, and deal with the very real possibility of failure.

It takes courage to transition. When the disciples witnessed Jesus walking on water, they became afraid, claiming it was a ghost. They began to cry and became gripped with fear. But Jesus immediately commanded them to, *"Take courage!"* (Matthew 14:27). Similarly, when God called Joshua to lead the children of Israel after the death of Moses, He repeatedly commanded Joshua to, *"Be strong and courageous."* (Joshua 1). Transition requires courage. Courage is the ability to do something that frightens you. It is power under pressure, strength in the face of stress. We all possess it. For God has not given us the spirit of fear; but of power, and of love, and of a sound mind (2 Timothy 1:7). In times of transition, God commands us to *take* courage or *be* courageous. He commands us to exercise an ability that He already put in us when He created us. Essentially, when God calls us to transition, He is saying *get a grip and get going!*

Accordingly, Peter took heed to Christ's command, took courage, and transitioned out of the boat and onto the water. One foot at a time, he stepped out of the comfort zone of the boat and onto the sea in the midst of a storm. Christ's invitation to, "Come," outweighed Peter's fear of the raging winds and waves vying to take him out. The very same winds and waves were raging when he was in the safety of the boat. But Jesus' invitation to come out and do something great like walk on water, gave Peter the confidence he needed to go for it!

Jesus is calling all of us to step out of our comfort zones and walk on water with Him. The only difference between being in the boat (our comfort zone) and being out on the water (our destiny) is the proximity of Jesus. The closer you are to Christ, engaged in what He is doing, the closer you are to your destiny. With Christ ever close to us and living in us, when we step out of what makes us comfortable, we have the opportunity to see what God sees. We get a chance to do the unthinkable, to operate in and experience God's supernatural power. When we put our total trust in Him, we get to experience for ourselves God's love, grace, mercy, protection, and provision. He never said it would be easy. Christ invites us to step out of the boat despite the storms of life that come up against us. The bible says many are the afflictions of the righteous, but the Lord promises to deliver you from them all (Psalm 34:19).

Like Peter, as the storm rages we can allow fear to distract us, cause us to lose focus, and ultimately we will begin to sink. But just like the Lord rescued Peter from drowning, He will rescue us if we call on Him for help (Matthew 14:22-34). Equally, as in the case of the disciples that opted to stay in the boat, fear can cause us to miss out on opportunities of a lifetime. But although the other disciples were too afraid to step out of the boat, many of them went on to be used by God to turn the world upside down (Acts 17:6). God's purpose always prevails (Proverbs 19:21). Despite our limitations, weaknesses, or past mistakes, God works all things together for the good of those that love Him, who have been called according to His purpose (Romans 8:28).

I hear the Lord saying, *"it is time to train, transform, and transition"*. In other words, it is time to learn, change, and go!" The comfort zone is where we place limits on God and risk missing Him. It is time to step out of the boat and walk on the water. It is time to transition.

God showed me a generation of Kingdom Visionaries tasked with ushering in a new era of revival, a new era of creativity, and a new era of relational ministry. This new era will showcase the real glory of the cross depicted by the vertical incline of a heart surrendered to God and the outreached hand embracing the world that He so loved that He sent His only begotten Son to die for it. This generation of Kingdom Visionaries are sold out disciples of Jesus Christ with a revelation from God to complete a supernatural assignment in the earth realm.

For this generation of leaders in the Body of Christ, the old-school church got it wrong for far too long. This generation of leaders is saying no to divisions, distractions, religion, and tradition and is instead declaring a resounding YES to transition. If that is you, be encouraged and know that you are a Kingdom Visionary. You have experienced a shift in mindset as it relates to your life's purpose. At every level of transition God is drawing you closer and closer to Him and the vision is getting clearer and clearer. Where you use to be, the way you use to teach and learn the Word of God has shifted because you and your whole generation has changed.

As I studied for this chapter, I came across a powerful prophetic Word by Dr. Jonathan David. Dr. David said that, "the year 2010 was the end of the decade of destiny and now we are in the decade of acceleration". When I read this, God began to remind me where He had me in 2010. It was at that time I was born again and my pastor established her church. I submitted myself to leadership and to strict training in the Word, but I was not the only one. God revealed to me that across the nations there was a birthing of many young leaders, ministries, and apostolic movements. Dr. David prophesied back then, that a "quickening was coming, an anointing to mature and to take us up to the next level." He said, "From the nations of the world a new generation will arise. A new company of people will get ready for what is about to happen." I believe we are the generation that God was talking about through His prophet.

Kingdom Visionaries are feeling the urgency in the spirit to birth, to accomplish their assignment, to walk in their purpose. You have trained on the Word of God, the Holy Spirit has transformed you by the renewing of your mind, and the eyes of your heart have been illuminated. You have been receiving more and more vision. You are dreaming bigger. Sometimes it does not make financial sense or there is no direct plan for you to obtain it, but you have caught God's vision for your life, your family, for your ministry, and you know that God is calling you higher!

God has released a major outpouring of purpose in the hearts of His chosen as a sign of a dawning of a new day, a fresh wind, the rise of peculiar leaders, Kingdom Visionaries seemingly coming from nowhere. In this decade of acceleration, leaders are being activated, not by a church building, a title, or a uniform, but are being activated by the anointing. God is revealing His glory to this generation! If you received a revelation of the glory of God living on the inside of you, I am here to tell you that this is your season to transition. I repeat, this is your season to transition.

CHAPTER ELEVEN

WHAT IS TRANSITION

What is transition? Simply put, transition is to move, shift, switch, evolve. It is the period by which you move from one state or condition to another. For example, in adolescence you transition from middle school to high school, from high school to whatever comes next. You then transition from living at home to living outside of the family cocoon, or from the safety of a college campus out into the world of independent living and work. Life transitions come at many junctures in a lifetime. They may arrive as graduations, job changes, weddings, births of children, deaths of parents and other loved ones, marriage problems, divorce, war, natural disasters, sudden shifts into wealth or fame, bankruptcy, sudden weight loss, a new body, or, as in my case, a move to a new city.

Transitions are never comfortable, but they are a fact of life and the will of God. Jesus went through many painful transitions in life. The Bible tells us that He was, *"A Man of sorrows and acquainted with grief."* (Isaiah 53:3). But the sorrow He experienced in the Garden of Gethsemane on the night before His crucifixion seemed to be the culmination of all the sorrow He had ever known. In Mark 14, Jesus says to His closest disciples, *"My soul is exceedingly sorrowful, even to death. Stay here and watch."* In times of transition you can feel lonely. You tend to feel abandoned by your friends and family, and even abandoned by God. You find it hard to comprehend or even submit to the will of God for your life. Jesus went through that as He suffered at Gethsemane. The very word Gethsemane means olive press. Olives were pressed there to make oil, and truly, Jesus was being pressed from all sides so that the Holy Spirit could be poured out on those who believe in Him.

I do not think we can even begin to fathom what Christ was going through in that Garden. Jesus prayed that if it were possible the cup of suffering would be taken from Him, but that the will of the Father would nevertheless be done. He prayed so fervently, and in such agony of spirit that his sweat fell to the ground like great drops of blood (Luke 22:44).

Though it was an incomprehensibly painful, horrific transition, it was necessary for the ultimate goal of what was accomplished. Jesus transitioned through Gethsemane and ultimately to the cross, so that now we can call upon His name. In times of transition you have your will, you know what you want. Yet, you can sense that God's will is at work and that He is up to something. In those times, all you can do is hold on to the vision God gave you just as Christ did. Hebrews 12 says He *"endured the cross, scorning its shame,"* and He did this *"for the joy that was set before Him."* Jesus knew that He would have great joy on the other side of the suffering and so will we.

One thing certain about transition is that it does not allow you to stay in the same place. You can fight it all you want, but life will let you know that it is time and until you transition to the next level, you will be miserable. Even if the assignment seems too daunting, we must be like Christ and surrender to God's will for our lives. The Word of God says that we are transforming into the image of Christ from glory to glory. That means that with an ever-increasing glory, we are becoming more and more like the Son.

As we change and transform into the new, our old

environments, our old behaviors, our old relationships, our old mindsets can no longer accommodate the new us. Accordingly, God allows circumstances to occur in our lives to get us to move, to shift, to transition into new experiences, new opportunities, new revelation, new dimensions, because God makes all things new!

Transitions are complicated, they are emotionally challenging, sometimes downright painful, sometimes exciting, but these are important times for us to focus on the then, the now, and the new. In other words, God uses transitions to help us assess the past, embrace the present, and move on to the future.

For example, I remember when I was single I had this really cute pair of jeans. I wore those jeans every chance I got! They fit me real nice too. I could pair those jeans with a cute blouse and some heels or with a nice t-shirt and flats, and look really good. I loved those jeans. But then I got married. Praise God I married a man that loves to cook. My heart was happy, my belly was full, and I started gaining some weight. My body started changing. And now, when I tried to put on my favorite pair of jeans, there began to be fight, a tussle, a struggle to get them on my new body.

Now, if I got them on, I could hardly breath. But that did not stop me from trying again the next time, all the while my hips kept getting wider and wider. I would try to put on my favorite pair of jeans and after the fight, the tussle, and the struggle, now the jeans could not get past my knees. At that moment something became crystal clear to me, I could not fit those jeans anymore! Now, I had to make a decision. I figured I could go on a diet, lose the weight, and get back into those old jeans. Or I could let go of the past, keep eating good, and go shopping for some new jeans. How many of you know which way I landed on that decision? That is right, I am eating good and I hired a stylist to keep me looking cute in some new jeans!

As you can see in the natural, the more I ate, the more my body transformed, it grew, it changed and in turn, I had to transition past my old jeans and into a new pair. Let us take a look at this in the spiritual. As you feed on the Word of God, your spirit begins to transform, it begins to grow. Accordingly, you will have to transition from your past in order to accommodate the new you. So, as your spirit transforms, you will begin yearning for something more, something different, something new. The new you will require you to transition past your old fleshly desires, past old relationships, past old environments. Just like there was a fight to get my new body into those old jeans, there will be a fight between the flesh and the Spirit to transition forward to the new thing God has for you.

For many leaders in the Body of Christ, you feel this frustration in the spirit. The frustration you are feeling in the spirit is not a bad frustration. It is good frustration. You have a lack of satisfaction. Something in you is desiring for more. It is like growing pains, a fight, a tussle and a struggle in your spirit. There is frustration in your spirit because your spirit knows that it is time to go. It is time to transition. You have trained and you have transformed. You are not the same person you used to be and these spiritual growing pains are intensifying. God is trying to tell you that it is time to transition. That is the only way the frustration is going to subside. In this season, you must lay hold to where God is taking you and then move.

Transitions are moments of leaving a past that has been reasonably steady and familiar for a future that will inevitably be different. In times of transition, now creates controversy. Now creates conflict, the struggle, and the fight. Now is the bridge between that long-standing regular and familiar past and the irregular, strange and unpredictable future. The now bridge may be short and shaky, long and hard, or anywhere in between. But when God leads you to a place of transition and you find yourself standing on the now bridge, you are likely going to have to tackle two equally challenging realities:

1) Letting go of the past and

2) embracing the future.

Any time you are in a state of transition in your life and God is calling on you to move, you will have to let go of your past in order to move effectively into your future.

CHAPTER TWELVE

DON'T LOOK BACK

To help me explain this even better, the Holy Spirit reminded me of a simple scripture found in Luke 17:32, where Jesus cautions us to, *"Remember Lot's wife."* This is the 2nd shortest scripture in the bible and I realized it was really quite profound as I began to study it. The New Living Translation illustrates a more passionate plea from our Lord and with great intensity ending with an exclamation point, He decrees, *"Remember what happened to Lot's wife!"* To understand why this scripture is so important and relates so well to what we are talking about, let me quickly remind you who Lot's wife was.

The original story, of course, comes to us from Genesis chapter 19, out of the days of Sodom and Gomorrah. The Lord could not stand all the evil that was going on and told Lot and his family to flee because those cities were about to be destroyed. The angel of the Lord said, "Flee for your lives! Don't look back..." After some negotiation with the angel, Lot and his family took their time and waited until morning to leave. But when they left, verse 24 says, *"Then the Lord rained down burning sulfur on Sodom and Gomorrah – from the Lord out of the heavens. Thus he overthrew those cities and the entire plain, destroying all..."* Now in the next verse is where we find my point. Verse 26 says, *"But Lot's wife looked back..."* Now the Lord clearly instructed them "don't look back", but Lot's wife, the bible says, *"looked back, and she became a pillar of salt."*

One of the purposes of history is to teach us the lessons of life. Marcus Garvey, famous civil rights activist, says, *"A people without the knowledge of their past history, origin, and culture is like a tree without roots."* The great philosopher, George Santayana, said, *"Those who cannot remember the past are condemned to repeat it."* So, if the past is this important—and it surely is—what was so wrong with Lot's wife looking back? Apparently, what was wrong with Lot's wife was that she was not just looking back, in her heart she wanted to go back. It would appear that even before they were past the city limits she was already missing what Sodom and Gomorrah had offered her. Though Sodom was overflowing with sin and vice, apparently the dark and oppressive city was comfortably familiar to Lot's wife.

I think back on where most of my friends and I came from. We grew up in the city streets, poor, surrounded by crime, drugs, sex, and violence. Some of us made it out, went on to do great things in life. But some of us did not, instead finding it difficult to leave the familiar behind. We have all heard the saying, *you can take the girl out of the hood, but you can't take the hood out of the girl.* That saying is as true today as it was in the days of Sodom and Gomorrah's destruction. Even when God Himself says to us, "It is time to move on," letting go of the familiar is tough and for Lot's wife it proved fatal.

You see, the past is to be learned from, but not lived in. There is nothing wrong with revisiting and reflecting carefully on all the experiences of our lives, the situations we have encountered, things we have been through or have been involved in and to draw from them the lessons that God wants us to learn from them. Lot's wife was not able to let go of her home in Sodom, even though God sent angels to warn her family to run for their lives because judgment was coming. The angels commanded them saying, "Don't look back" and "don't stop." So, it is not just that she looked back, she did so while longing to return.

Please take heed, Kingdom Visionaries. When you have the lessons, now it is time to transition. Now it is time to move forward on to the future. We must remember that faith is always pointed toward the future. Faith always operates in the now. *Now faith is the substance of things hoped for, the evidence of things not seen* (Hebrews 11:1). So, a better way to talk about Lot's wife is to say that she did not have faith. Her attachment to the past outweighed her confidence in the future. She doubted God's ability to give her something better than what she already had. Apparently, she thought—fatally, as it turned out—that nothing that lay ahead could possibly be as good as those things she was leaving behind. But, God is looking for His Kingdom Visionaries to stand on some now faith, move forward, and not look back!

Are you yearning to return to the old you or to old places, old faces, or back to a world that cannot be lived in now? Are you constantly dissatisfied with the new you or your present circumstances? Do you have only a sad view of the future? Do you miss the here-and-now-and-tomorrow because you are so trapped in the there-and-then-and-yesterday? Well, Jesus says in Luke 9:62, *"No one who puts his hand to the plow and looks back is fit for service in the kingdom of God."* So, if you are struggling with a destructive habit or find yourself yielding to the temptation to turn back just one more time, for one last look, one last taste, one last fix—even as God whispers, "Don't look back! Transition, move, go forth"—these were some of the sins of Lot's wife and Jesus is cautioning us to remember her.

When Jesus warns us to, *"Remember Lot's wife"*, what He is really saying is, *"Have faith in God"* (Mark 11:22). Faith is for the future. Faith builds on the past, but never longs to stay there. Faith trusts that God has great things in store for you because He knows the plans He has for you. God's plan is good and it is intended to give you a future and a hope (Jeremiah 29:11). Ask yourself, "Where is my faith?" Is it stuck in your past? If so, that is not genuine faith. Faith is now. Faith moves. Faith is active. We are called to walk by faith which signifies that faith is a forward motion. So, no matter what it looks like, no matter the storms, no matter the trials or tribulations, we can "count it all joy" because we see things through the lens of our faith and we believe in a God that loves us and wants the best for us.

From God's point of view, everything is connected. God works all things together for the good. He wants us to remember the things that happened in the past because as we walk with Him, He is sure to give us a powerful testimony of deliverance. Our testimony will always reveal something more about the God we serve; His character, nature, and attributes. We would remember Him making a way out of no way. We would recall being snatched out of defeat and lifted up to victory. We remember how He made impossible situations possible. Then, going forward, we would have the confidence and trust we need to remind us that God never leaves nor forsakes us (Deuteronomy 31:6).

This is your season to transition! The Lord is creating situations in your life where you have to apply monumental faith to see God move in your life. For most of us, where God is taking us is so new and unfamiliar that we have to be ok with throwing our hands up in the air and saying, "I can't explain where God is taking me, but I'm ok with it." Do not be afraid to make big jumps even when it makes no financial or strategic sense. If you feel the leading of the Lord toward a certain way, you need to know that there is grace for large leaps of faith. This may mean geographical moves for you and your family. Moves from a particular ministry or you might have to shut down your church or business and start over. This could even mean breaking off certain relationships or unholy ties with those you have been well connected to. God is sending you out to connect with people that have the kind of faith that scares you. But God says fear nothing, because I am with you! Transition by faith.

CHAPTER THIRTEEN

TRANSITION BY FAITH

The story of David illustrates a life of faith and transition. He started as a little lad who tended his father's sheep. David went through some trying experiences in the pasture that would have been difficult for him if he did not have faith. However, God proved Himself to young David and he was able to transition forward by faith. So, when Israel had problems with a Philistine giant, David remembered God's past victories in the pasture, embraced the present challenge before him, and transitioned forward by faith and overcame the giant ahead of him.

In another very familiar passage of Psalms 23, David illustrates how to transition by faith. In these six verses of Psalm 23, we see some powerful and precious promises as we transition through life. David transitions from being just Jesse's son, to shepherd boy, to warrior, to King of Israel. David writes in verse 1 of Psalm 23, *"The Lord is my shepherd, I lack nothing."* Here, David is reflecting on his time as a shepherd and relates those experiences to his relationship with God, declaring that the Lord is his shepherd. *"He makes me lie down in green pastures, he leads me beside quiet waters, he refreshes my soul. He guides me along the right paths for his name's sake."* These verses show God's care for us as a shepherd, providing for us as we transition through life on the path to our destiny.

In verse 4, David, in transition, says, *"Even when I walk through the darkest valley, I will not be afraid, for you are close beside me."* The New King James Version says, *"Yea though I walk through the valley of the shadow of death, I will fear no evil: for You are with me; Your rod and Your staff, they comfort me."* God calls us to transition even when it looks dark and dead. Whether it is the ending of something we thought would last forever, or a crossroad where we are forced to make decisions we feel we are not prepared to make, or a new beginning that challenges us to move out of our comfort zones, we must transition by faith.

You must declare like David did, "I am walking <u>through</u> this valley. This dark place can't stop me, this dead place can't hold me." Isaiah 43:2 says, *"When you pass through the waters, I will be with you; and through the rivers, they shall not overwhelm you; when you walk through the fire you shall not be burned, and the flame shall not consume you."* So, you ought to stand on the promises of God and go, move, transition <u>through</u>!

Observe the key word and the repetition of the word "through" in that verse. Through means transition. Through means forward motion. When you transition through you know that it is not a permanent place, it is just a passage way. Realize today, that the valley is not a permanent place. Dark, but not permanent. Painful, but not permanent. Stressful, but not a permanent. Do not focus on what you are going through, rather, celebrate the fact that God is taking you through! And because God is with you, you will not be overwhelmed, you will not be burned, you will not be consumed! So, transition by faith!

David says, *"I fear no evil, for You are with me"*. In transition, you have the promise of God's presence. In transition, when you are put into a place of hardship where none of your friends can rescue you, when your finances cannot make a way for you and the things that used to be at your disposal are now gone, in your frustration, you may even ask, "Where is God?" because He is all you have left. The very place you perceive to be the worse place to be is actually the best place you can ever be. Why? Because when God wants you to transition, He shows up every time! In transition, you get a revelation of who God is. In transition, God reveals His glory to you because that is what you are going to need in order to move forward! Transition is hard, but since you are transitioning according to God's will, there is nothing that you cannot overcome and conquer.

Your transition is the place where you come to realize that God is with you. Your transition is where you come to experience for yourself the power and purpose of God's presence. You will find that the same God who is with you in the good times, is the same God who is with you in the challenging times of your life. The same God who stands with you during the mountain top moments stands by you in the valleys of your life. The same God who blesses you with the bright times of your life is the same God who shows up in the midnight hour. The Lord promises us just as He promised Joshua, *"Be strong and courageous. Do not be afraid; do not be discouraged, for the Lord your God will be with you wherever you go."* (Joshua 1). Jesus said in Matthew

28:20, *"And surely I am with you always, to the very end of the age."* Hebrews 13:5, God said, *"Never will I leave you; never will I forsake you."* God is with you in every transition.

So why, even in knowing all of this, do so many of us fail to transition into the new? Why do we fail to move forward into our purpose? We train, we transform, but we do not transition onward in the direction toward the abundant life that God predestined for us. Even though we know what the Word says, even though He's proven faithful, even though our spirit is telling us this does not fit us anymore. Some people live all their lives going to church and never experiencing abundance. Their lives are filled with hardship. They reach just the bare minimum, settling for crumbs instead of the whole cake. Why? Because when it is time to transition they look back to the past and start remembering.

The past. It looks familiar. The pain is familiar. The hurt just makes sense. Dryness, darkness, despair, and even death becomes that overnight guest who just never left and has become a welcomed part of the family. Too often we look back, but fail to move forward. We do not want to give up on the security of the known because the insecurity of the unknown is just too much to process. We look back, but then we do not move into new opportunities that grow our capabilities. We look back, but we are not willing to take a chance that can expand our influence or leadership abilities. We look back, but remain stagnant, never willing to accept the challenges, never really learning to depend on God and His unconditional love for us.

We know that faith is the key that unlocks the door to God's storehouse of blessing, healing and provision. If Satan can cause us to doubt and hinder our faith, then he has the victory. Satan always looks for that foothold in our lives that he could fill up with doubt. Doubt is a sin which so easily ensnares many of us. The enemy uses doubt to try and keep us from seeing by faith what God promised us in His Word. But I am here to remind you that the devil is a liar. This is your season for transition. All it takes is faith and vision.

CHAPTER FOURTEEN

FAITH AND VISION

Repeat after me: *"All it takes is faith and vision. All it takes is faith and vision. All it takes is faith and vision."* Let me remind you of what vision is. Proverbs 29:18 says, *"Where there is no vision, the people perish..."* The word vision means revelation. Revelation means something that is revealed or communicated by God to humans; or the divine or supernatural disclosure of truth. God wants us to see the invisible (2 Corinthians 4:18). The unseen is eternal, which means there are no limits to what God wants to reveal to His people! God wants us to have a vision of the Kingdom of Heaven, because that is where our blessings are manifested. We have already been blessed with all spiritual blessings in heavenly places (Ephesians 1:3). Bishop T.D. Jakes says, "If you can conceive the invisible, you can achieve the impossible. Conceive means to visualize, picture, or see a thing. Vision enables us to see the invisible.

Our vision of God keeps us going when everything seems like it is falling apart all around us. It is the vision of God and His Kingdom that is where we find strength to keep going. That is why God tells us to set our *"minds on things above, not on earthly things"* (Colossians 3:2). That is what people of faith do. When we consider the *Hall of Fame of Faith* in Hebrews 11, from Abel, Enoch, Noah, Abraham, Sarah, etc., verse 13 says, *"All these people were still living by faith when they died. They did not receive the things promised; they only saw them and welcomed them from a distance, admitting that they were foreigners and strangers on earth."* Kingdom Visionaries are people of faith and vision. Like these men and women of faith, you must hold on to the vision that God has given you and never lose sight of it. Faith is the substance of things hoped for and the evidence of the unseen (Hebrews 11:1).

P.K. Bernard said, "A man without a vision is a man without a future. A man without a future will always return to his past." We see how, in John 21, Peter was discouraged and did not know what to do after the tragedy of Jesus' death. So, Peter declared in vs. 3, *"I'm going fishing."* In other words, *I'm going back to what I'm good at and what I know, and that's fishing.* The Israelites did the same thing when God used Moses to bring them out of Egypt after four hundred years of slavery. They wanted to go back to Egypt, preferring slavery over freedom. They settled for what they could see rather than transitioning forward to what they could not see.

Let us look at the transition of a man who had faith and vision. In Mark 10:46, we see the story of blind Bartimaeus. Bartimaeus was on the road begging as usual, but on this day, he heard Jesus was passing through. Verse 47 says that Bartimaeus simply heard it was Jesus and immediately he knew it was his time for transition. It was his moment to make a move. He shouted, *"Jesus, have mercy on me."* In verse 48 we see his opposition telling him to be quiet. However, in their attempt to quiet him, Bartimaeus became even more indignant and cried even louder, *"Son of David have mercy on me!"* Now, this particular cry was a cry of faith. By this cry, Bartimaeus had declared Jesus as the Son of David, which meant he believed that Jesus was the Son of God, the promised Savior of Israel. The cry of blind Bartimaeus caught Jesus' attention. When Jesus heard this cry, verse 49 says Jesus stood still and called

Bartimaeus to Himself.

This is a beautiful picture of salvation. One day we too heard about Jesus and we responded by faith crying, "Son of God, have mercy on me!" And Jesus stopped everything to call us to Himself! *Selah.*

When blind Bartimaeus answered the call, he moved, shifted, and transitioned to his destiny. The bible says, in verse 50, that he threw aside his garment, rose and came to Jesus. When Bartimaeus moved and threw aside his begging garment, it signified the letting go of the old and transitioning forward on to something new. Blind Bartimaeus was different because he was called. He was called and he was transformed, so now he had to transition! When Bartimaeus got to the Savior, Jesus asked him, *"What can I do for you?"* Bartimaeus asked the Lord for his sight. But notice the key to this man receiving his healing. In verse 52, Jesus said, *"Go, your faith has healed you."* Bartimaeus was transformed and immediately began to bear the fruit of his transformation. He transitioned to something new. In his transformed state, he did not go back to sitting on the road begging. That was no longer befitting of a man called and healed by God.

Do not miss this: The Bible says that when Bartimaeus received his sight, he immediately transitioned down the road following Jesus! After he was called, he was healed, now he transitioned forward toward Jesus. Wow! You see, the fruit or the evidence of your training is your transformation. Accordingly, the fruit or the evidence of your transformation is your transition. It is the audacity of transformation. You change just so everything around you has got to change. It is like we have no choice, we have to move, to shift, to transition. The old place just does not fit anymore! Your transformation requires a shifting in the atmosphere. Your transformation requires your transition! Bartimaeus was transformed. He was called. He was healed. And so he transitioned on the road following Jesus.

Do you know that the road to Jesus is a narrow road? It is a slim, tight, and a restricted road. Mathew 7:24, says, *"Small is the gate and narrow the road that leads to life, and only a few find it."* Only a few find it because your opposition will make it difficult for you. Your pride will oppose you, your sin, haters, fear, and doubt and all the forces of satan will oppose you. The world system will battle against you and try to stop you from transitioning on the road to your purpose, to your destiny, and on to eternity. But it is only on that narrow road that you will find life.

Jesus came that you may have life and have it more abundantly (John 10:10). Jesus tells us, in Luke 13:24, to *"Strive to enter through the narrow gate, for many, I say to you, will seek to enter and will not be able."* Jesus says to strive, in other words, endeavor, go all out, do your best, pull out all the stops, make every effort to transition through the narrow gate and find the narrow road.

I am reminded of the Apostle Paul, who was also on a road when he met Jesus. Paul was in transition. He was on the road to Damascus going to persecute believers (Acts 9). Paul, who was Saul then, was very religious. He was a good Pharisee who knew the Law and sincerely believed that the Christian movement was dangerous to Judaism. He hated Christians and felt justified in persecuting them without mercy. In fact, he felt like he was doing God a favor by getting rid of these crazy people who talked about a man named Jesus Christ who had risen from the dead. Kingdom Visionaries, if you are not careful, you can find yourself transitioning down the wrong road. Proverbs 14:12 says, *"There is a path before each person that seems right, but it ends in death."*

Bartimaeus was on the road blind physically, but could see Jesus in his heart. Paul however, had the benefit of physical sight but he was blind spiritually. Bartimaeus encounters Jesus and immediately gains his sight. But Jesus encounters Paul and takes away his eyesight. So, Paul is blinded to the world so God can open the eyes of his heart through the Gospel. Paul's sight is regained only when Ananias teaches Paul the Gospel, because faith comes by hearing and hearing by the word of God (Romans 10:17).

When Paul believes by faith, Acts 9:18 says, *"And immediately something like scales fell from his eyes, and his sight was restored. Then he got up and was baptized."* When Paul believed by faith on Jesus Christ, the scales fell from his eyes, and he had vision. Once Paul could see, he got up, transitioned forward and was baptized into the Body of Christ. So, in order to transition down the right road, in order to transition through the right gate, not only do you need faith to get on the road, but you have to be able to see where you are going. Jesus says, *"I am the gate; whoever enters through me will be saved. They will come in and go out, and find good pasture."* (John 10:9). But can you see the gate?

Sometimes we experience moments of blurred vision, times in life where we lose perspective, where we just cannot see God in the circumstance. Circumstances where disappointment, despair, doubt, and disillusionment can cause us to lose sight of our Savior. We literally fail to see what is right before our very eyes. We are like the two disciples on the Emmaus road in Luke 24:13-35. They could not even see Jesus walking alongside them due to discouragement and a lack of faith. Despite Jesus having told them what would take place, despite having been told that the women had both seen angels and the risen Christ, the disciples could not see beyond what the natural eye could reveal.

According to John 16:13, the Holy Spirit will guide us into all truth. He will literally show us things to come. The proper sense of the verb 'show' is "to cause a person to see." In other words, the Spirit of God directs, steers, and points us to the truth and the Holy Spirit also enables us to see that truth and what is to come in the future! The Holy Spirit leads us to the light and cuts the light on. That is called spiritual illumination. Spiritual illumination is the process by which the Holy Spirit helps a person to understand the truth of God's Word. The Holy Spirit helps us to understand the revelation, He helps us to capture the vision. This means we need to pray to the Lord, *"Open my eyes that I may see wonderful things in your law."* (Psalm 119:18). Every believer should pray this prayer by faith every time we attempt to read God's Word. Our eyes must be opened to see the vision God has for us.

Take a moment and lift your hands to Heaven as an act of surrender, and from a sincere heart, pray: *"Lord, I want to see. Open my eyes that I may see wonderful things in your law. I want to see the gate and the narrow road to life. I know only a few will find it. Many are called but only a few are chosen. Lord, here I am. Choose me, I'll go. Enlighten the eyes of my heart. I want to see You. I want to know You. Build up my faith. Sharpen my vision. Work within me. Give me the desire and the power to do all that pleases You. In Jesus' name. Amen.*

For many of you, God has given you a vision, but you need clarity about the vision. God has told you where to go, but you feel the need for more direction on which way to go. Your heart has been stirred because all you need are the plans and the strategies. I have good news for you, the plans and the strategies are being released to you in this season because it is time to transition. Intensify fasting and prayer and watch how much more clarity begins to roll into your viewpoint. Press into the very presence of God and listen to His still small voice. In this season, God is yelling the vision, but He is whispering the strategies.

Kingdom Essential: A key strategy in this season is collaboration. Kingdom Visionaries do not compete, they collaborate. The Lord is telling us to pay attention to divine connections and partnerships. It is time to invite intercessors that you know and trust to begin to pray for you and your ministry. In Genesis 11:6 the Lord said, *"If as one people speaking the same language they have begun to do this, then nothing they plan to do will be impossible for them."* We need one another.

In this season, we must transition in unity, as a team, with Christ as the Head and not ourselves. It is not about making a name for yourself. One of the things that God has been calling you to fight as a leader is your own fleshly ambitions. This is one of the greatest *tests* for leaders, or as translated in the Greek, 'temptations.' We are constantly tempted in the area of our desire for greatness. But our desire for greatness must be intended to make God's kingdom greater. As leaders, we have to discern when it is our own ambition versus when it is the

Lord's ambition in us. God calls us to greater, He calls us to be great, but it is a call according to His purpose and not our own. So, do not be afraid to transition when God gives you a large platform, just beware of *you* becoming the large platform.

Let us examine Paul's transition into his role as Apostle. Ephesians chapter 3 illustrates his humility. Paul is overwhelmed that God chose him, one who had previously persecuted Christians unto death, to preach the Gospel to the Gentiles. Paul declares that he is *"less than the least of all God's people."* These are not words of pride. He refers to himself as a servant, not some high priest. He speaks of his ministry as God's grace given to him for the Gentiles, and he speaks of his strength to do so as God's power. He speaks of the message he brings as the *"unsearchable riches of Christ"* and the mystery that God made plain through the death and resurrection of Jesus Christ. Paul takes credit for nothing, yet Paul was an Apostle known throughout the world, a preacher who brought hundreds to Christ everywhere he went. Paul was not keeping count. He was not counting the likes, followers, or fans. He was simply faithful to his assignment.

Philippians 3:9-10 says that Paul's great ambition in life is to

"...be found in him". In other words, he must come to know Christ by coming to know the power of His resurrection and the fellowship of His sufferings, being conformed to His death. Knowing Christ like that, experiencing Christ on that level, transitioning through life in Christ if, by any means, verse 11 says, *"I may attain to the resurrection from the dead."* In our transition, we will come to know Christ. Like I told you before, we will know His sufferings by going through suffering. We will experience His death by going through deadly conditions. But we can rejoice in the fact that because Christ was resurrected from the dead, He has the power to raise us up from any dead place in our lives.

I want to encourage you today. At one time, you may have allowed fear and doubt to creep into your life and it overwhelmed you to the point where it was like rust rotting on iron. It started off small, but now it has spread all over your heart and you feel like you are spiritually dying. You feel the need to transition, to move and go higher, but things are just not working out. People may have turned their back on you, loved ones may have left you, and you may have even thought that God has rejected you. But I am here to let you know that the Lord has heard your cry! God is telling you today that you are not rejected, you are being resurrected. You need to begin to declare that over your life now! Say, "I am not rejected. I am being resurrected!"

The enemy wants to make you feel like a failure. He wants to make you feel like your stretch of ministry meant nothing and that you are heading nowhere. The devil, yet again, is a liar. Death could not hold Jesus. His glory lives on the inside of you. Therefore, death cannot hold you! God wants you to know that you are in transition. You are on the right road. You will not fail, you will not stay stagnant, you will not go back. You are in transition and you must experience the resurrection power of God because He is about to use you on a greater level. Dry your eyes and be encouraged. You thought the Lord did not hear you, but He did. He did not reject you, He is resurrecting you. Say it one more time, "I am not rejected. I am being resurrected."

Paul says, *"I want to know and experience the resurrection power of Jesus Christ."* Paul then says in Philippians 3: 13-14, *"Brethren, I count not myself to have apprehended: but this one thing I do, forgetting those things which are behind, and reaching forth unto those things which are before, I press toward the mark for the prize of the high calling of God in Christ*

Jesus." In this point of this journey, Paul wrote this letter as a prisoner in Rome. Yet he still saw the importance of pressing on to possess that perfection for which Christ Jesus first possessed him. He pressed toward the mark for the prize of the high calling of God in Christ Jesus.

Watch this. Paul was in prison, but He pressed on. He could not change his present circumstances, but that did not stop him from fulfilling his purpose of spreading the gospel to the Gentiles. For two years Paul was imprisoned in Rome. But from prison he wrote the Book of Ephesians. From prison, he wrote the Book of Philippians. From prison, he wrote the Book of Colossians, Philemon, and maybe even Hebrews.

Ever felt like you were in a prison? Maybe you feel like you are in a prison in your marriage, a prison on your job, or you feel like you are confined or trapped by your past or present circumstances. I am here to let you know that you can still press on, you can press toward the mark. In other words, transition on to your future. To do that, you are going to have to focus on the mark and forget what is behind you. You must focus and forget. What is God calling you to focus on, but you keep failing to do so? What is it that you should be forgetting, but you just cannot seem to let it go? To transition effectively, you must focus and forget.

CHAPTER FIFTEEN

FOCUS AND FORGET

Paul says, *"But this one thing I do."* He does not say these many things I do. Paul says this *one* thing I do. Paul was focused. He goes on to say, *"forgetting those things which are behind."* Paul also chose to forget.

He chose to forget the good. Paul had great successes and accomplishments. He was intelligent, a highly-educated Pharisee, a prolific writer and debater, but he had to forget those things less he became proud and arrogant. 2 Corinthians 12 tells us that to keep him humble, God put a thorn in Paul's flesh, a messenger from satan sent to torment him and keep him from becoming conceited. *"Take it away,"* Paul asked of the Lord three times. But each time God's answer was, *"My grace is sufficient for you, for my power is made prefect in weakness."* So, what does Paul do? He forgets all about it. He says in verse 9, *"Therefore I will boast all the more gladly about my weaknesses, so that Christ's power may rest on me."* Focus on the mark, and forget!

Paul chose to forget the bad. Before Paul got saved, he hated Christians. His mission, before encountering Jesus Christ, was to persecute the Church. His goal was to capture Christians and bring them to public trial and execution. But God! What have you done in your past that you are not proud of? The memories of all the bad things you have done and the sins of the past must be forgotten because God has forgiven you and He has forgotten them. Hebrews 8:12 says, *"For I will forgive their wickedness and will remember their sins no more."* 1 John 1:9 says, *"If we confess our sins, he is faithful and just to forgive us our sins, and to cleanse us from all unrighteousness."*

Take God at His Word. Confess your sin, forgive yourself, forgive others, and press on. Your Heavenly Father promises to restore you back to your proper place of fellowship with Him. We need to effectively train our brains to this truth through prayer and meditation on God's Word, *"Let this mind be in you which is also in Christ Jesus."* (Philippians 2:5). The Word of God gives us an assurance that we are no longer held hostage to who we used to be prior to salvation through Christ Jesus. If you fail to forgive yourself and fail to forget, then you will stay bound. You will continue to beat yourself up and let guilt hinder your progress. Romans 8:1 declares, *"Now there is no condemnation for those who belong to Christ Jesus."* In other words, if you have accepted Jesus Christ as your Lord and Savior, you are not condemned. You are free to forget.

Paul even had to forget the ugly. The bible tells us in 2 Corinthians 11:23 that Paul had been in prison more frequently, been flogged more severely, and been exposed to death again and again, more than any of the other Apostles. Paul was beaten with rods multiple times, shipwrecked three times, and stoned once. But he did not allow himself to dwell upon these things. He rarely mentions these hurts in his letters, and when he does, it is in his own defense as an Apostle. Paul did not wallow in the coulda, woulda, shoulda's. Whether it was the good, the bad, or the ugly, Paul says this one thing I do – forget.

Paul focuses, he forgets, and then he reaches forward, then he presses toward the mark (Philippians 3: 13-14). You have got to reach forward to those things which are ahead, Saints of God. The future will not just fall in your lap. You must stretch out and reach for it. Think about a runner with his eyes fixed firmly on the goal, his hands stretching out towards it, and his body bent forward as he moves swiftly towards the end of the race. Paul says, *"I press toward the mark."* The word "press" suggests strenuous effort being put forth. The runner keeps his eyes on the goal, the mark. There is a prize to be won and we must put forth every effort to obtain it. The prize is a high calling to final salvation where we are to be conformed to the image of the Son. We are all transitioning to eternal glory. We cannot afford to look back or stay stuck, we must press toward the prize!

Do not worry if no one gives you a nod of approval for your efforts. There may be those that go to extreme lengths to remind you of your past. God knows what you are doing, and that you are doing it for Him. Do not grow weary in well doing (Galatians 6:9). You can keep pressing because the Lord Almighty has set you free, and whom the Son sets free is free indeed (John 8:36). Forget those things that are behind you and reach forth to those things which are before you. Press toward the mark. Christ is the mark. He is our example, He is the Author and Finisher, the Pioneer and Perfector of our faith (Hebrews

12:2). Live each and every moment of each and every day for Jesus Christ. This is your season to transition. God is calling you higher.

And what do we do when the voice of discouragement seems to be so loud? We turn up the Word of the Lord. It is time to prophecy over yourself. Begin to declare what God has already told you about your future and your destiny. You may not have it all figured out yet and that is ok. As much as you know, begin to declare it in the name of Jesus! God is giving you a supernatural shift in your mind. God is removing those negative feelings that have been lingering over you about your future. God is saying my son, my daughter, now is the time. He is filling you with the strength and the fortitude to transition! Receive it!

I hear the Lord saying to His Kingdom Visionaries, *"It is time to train, transform, and transition. You must learn, change, and go. I have equipped you to think strategically. Therefore, come and let us reason together. My Word is a lamp unto your feet and a guide to your path. Do not fear. Your decisions are not rash, there is no room for regrets, for my glory has filled you. You are my temple. I dwell within you. I will work all things together for your good. As soon as you have thought it out and have decided for My Kingdom, put your hand on the plow and transition."*

Take heed to the Word of God given to you in these last days. Do not second-guess yourself into paralysis. If you look back, you will just mess the whole thing up. When you have determined the right thing to do, do it! Transition on to your platform. Go for it! That new job, take it! That promotion, take it! Birth the book, start the business, walk away from the old and into the new. Press into the stress of the new thing God has brought you into. Yes, it is uncomfortable, but stay the course. In most cases, it is not that you cannot do the job. It is more of the fact that you are transitioning into something new, something that you are not accustomed to. It is another level. But if you transition with a mindset focused on where you just left, it will cause the shift to be difficult. It will also cause your performance to be produced at a lesser standard than of what may be required. Moving out of one thing into another can bring agitation and in some cases rebellion. But I hear the Lord saying, *"Train. Transform. Transition."*

Train on God, self, and sphere. God will continue to transform you by the renewing of your mind, so that you can begin to see things differently and supernaturally. As you are continuously transformed into the image of the Son, you will be empowered to transition effectively into the life you deserve!

STRATEGIC TRAINING PLAN

Use this guide as a starting point for developing your personal strategic training plan. Strategic planning involves creating a mission (*See Train, Part 1*) and vision (*See Transform, Part 2*). To achieve the vision of God for your life, you must focus your training regimen on three strategic priorities: *God, self, and sphere*. These strategic priorities will determine how you will achieve the vision. Develop goals that target growth in the areas of God, self, and sphere. By making progress in these areas, and being faithful to the vision, we should expect to see transition (*See Transition, Part 3*) toward the life you deserve!

TRAIN TRANSFORM TRANSITION

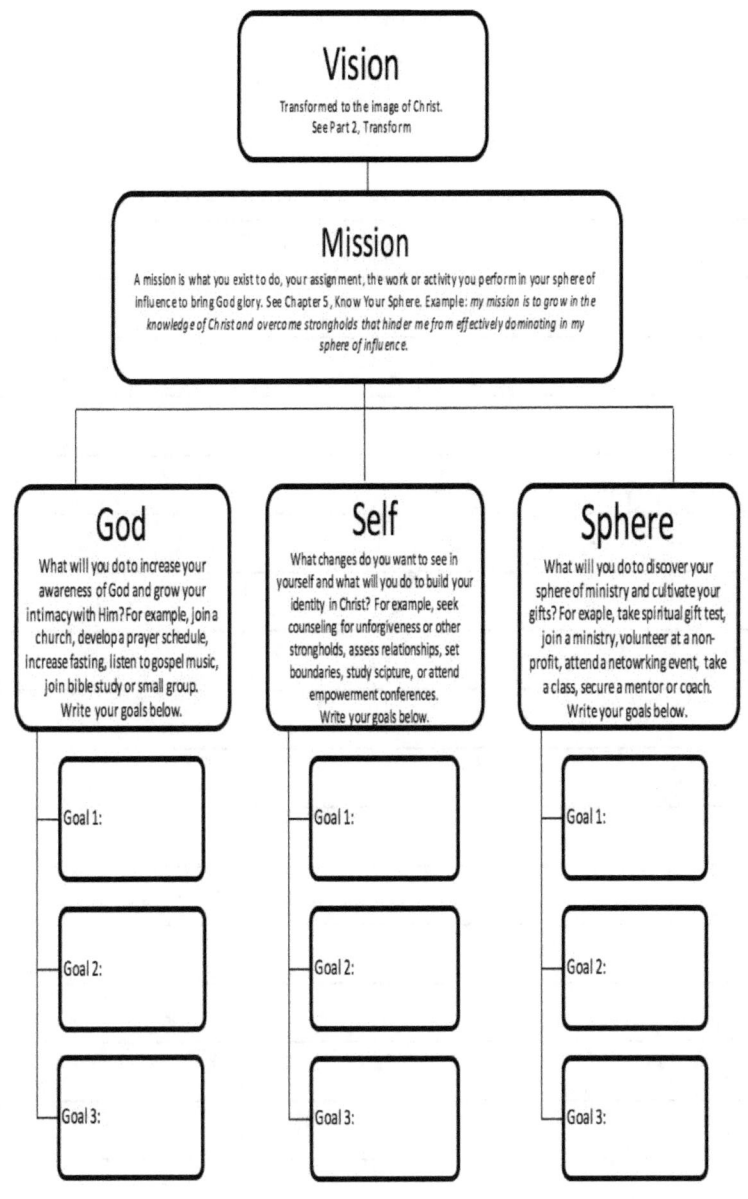

NOTES

TRAIN TRANSFORM TRANSITION

www.ingramcontent.com/pod-product-compliance
Lightning Source LLC
LaVergne TN
LVHW051559070426
835507LV00021B/2660